Mrs Mentary's Mystery Tours
London

Ellie Mentary

Lou + Rob,

I hope you've had the most amazing xmas ... I wanted to wish you an incredible 2025 and share with you Cathy's book of London Museums in place of a xmas card this year.

I do hope you and the family are keeping well and let's make sure that lunch happens sometime soon.

Much love, James, Katie, Thomas, Sophia, Luce + Emily

xxx

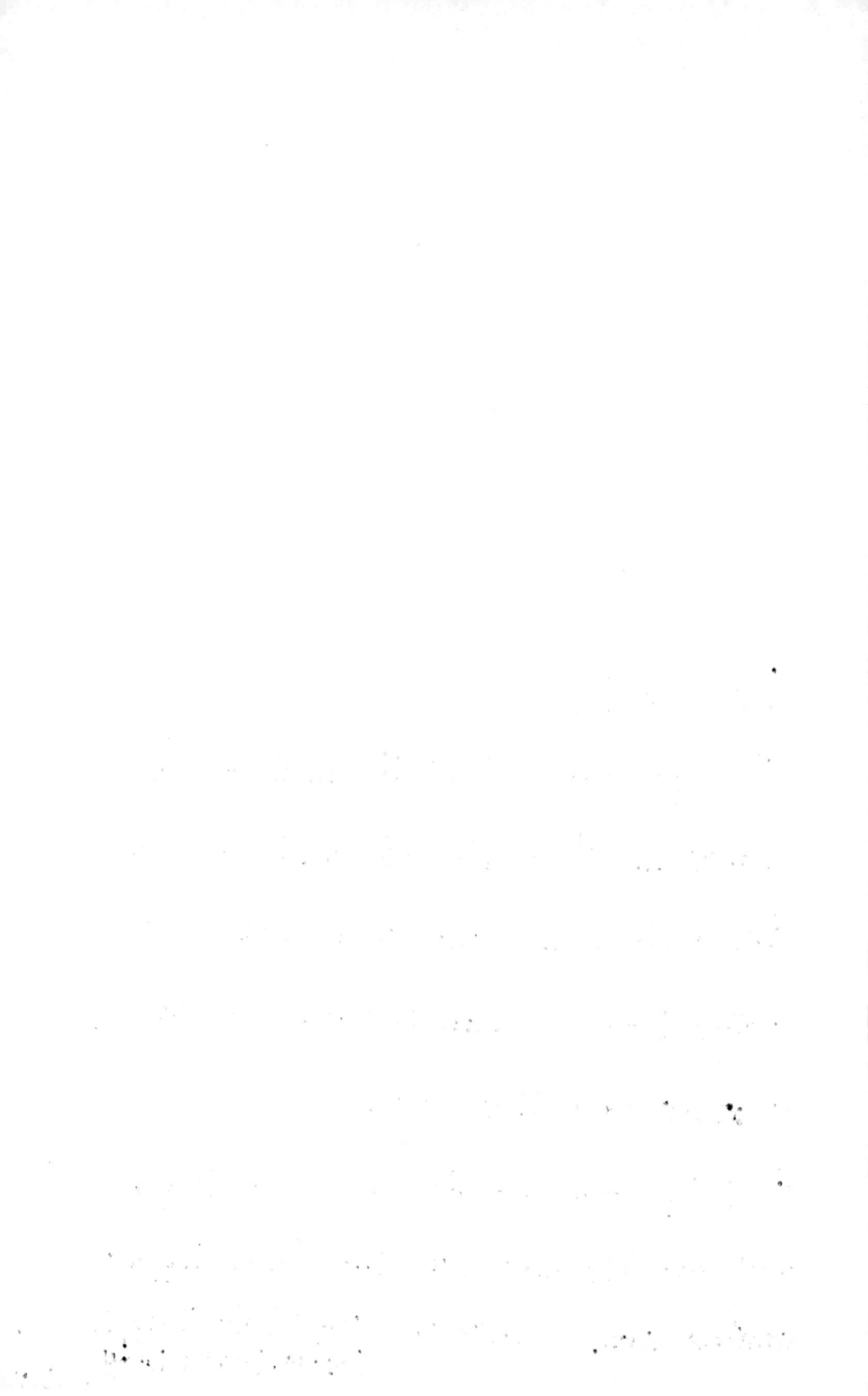

Contents

Book Cover by Thingkazupa

Published with Amazon KPD.

First edition 2024

Introduction

The start of your new adventure!

Mrs Eloise "Ellie" Mentary, freelance journalist and amateur sleuth, is a massive fan of two things - beautiful places and puzzles - so this book combines the two! London is a hugely popular tourist destination with national and international visitors enjoying the wealth of palaces, museums and parks on offer. A first time trip to London is likely to include a trip to Buckingham Palace, the London Eye, the Tower of London, Southbank, the British Museum and Harrods. However, this book focuses on some of the less well-known "villages" of London covering a wide range of different areas from the riverside wharfs and cobbled streets of Wapping, delightful markets in the area around London Bridge, fine period houses and green spaces of Hampstead and trendy graffiti covered warehouses of Hackney Wick. These areas are where the locals go for great food, shopping and soaking up the atmosphere to escape the crowds in central London.

The mystery tours are designed to help you get to know these lovely destinations whilst adding a bit of a mental challenge at the same time. If you like escape rooms, crosswords or logic puzzles you will really enjoy the brainteaser element to the tours. During the pandemic Mrs Mentary put together mystery tours for her family when nothing was open and they really enjoyed exploring their local area. In these cost conscious times the book offers some free (once you've bought the book!) entertainment which will hopefully get people enjoying the outdoors and opening their eyes to some of the beauty on their doorstep.

For all clues you are looking for some sort of object or place which will help you eliminate one of the suspects. The clues are somewhat cryptic with certain words having double meanings. To help you significant words are italicised. You will start to learn certain phrases that mean "anagram" or "contained within" etc so look out for those. Also remember that words may have different meanings in different contexts. If you get stuck on a clue the best thing is to take a photo of the relevant place or object and go back to the clue once you have eliminated most of the suspects. The tours are generally within two and three miles long and take around one and a half to two hours if you were to do them from start to finish without a break. However, there are lots of lovely shops, pubs and restaurants along most of the routes so you may well want to make a half-day or day of it.

The book also contains a list of places to eat, shop and visit in each location. Places do close or change periodically so if anything is out of date please do let Mrs Mentary know so she can update for future editions. In addition, check out some of the following websites and Instagram accounts for fantastic information on the latest in hotels, restaurants, shops and attractions:

www.timeout.com

www.visitlondon.com

www.londonist.com

www.secretldn.com

www.muddystilettos.co.uk

www.coolplaces.co.uk

www.cntraveller.com

www.wherecanwego.com

@volga_londonstories

Please do take photos of your experiences on the tours and share with others (though please do not give away the answers to any of the clues..)

Ellie Mentary

Mrs Mentary's Mystery Tours
www.mrsmentarysmysterytours.co.uk
Email: enquiries@mrsmentarysmysterytours.com
Instagram: @mrsmentarysmysterytours
Facebook page

Map

Location of Mystery Tours in London around the River Thames.

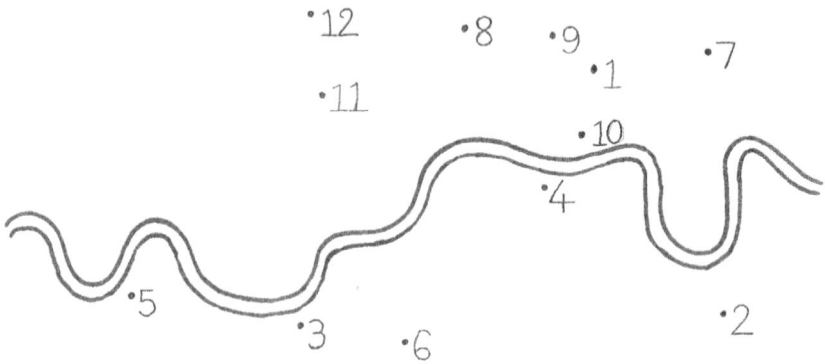

1. Victoria Park and Bethnal Green, 2. Blackheath, 3. Wandsworth, 4. Bermondsey Street, Maltby Street Market and Borough Market, 5. Barnes, 6. Clapham, 7. Stratford and Hackney Wick, 8. Highbury and Canonbury, 9. Broadway Market and Hackney, 10. Wapping, 11. Belsize Park, 12. Hampstead

Tour One - Victoria Park and Bethnal Green

Miniatures and Misdemeanours

I t was a frosty day in January and Mrs Mentary was visiting the V&A Museum of Childhood in Bethnal Green to report on a dolls house furniture competition. Artists and craftsmen from all over the country had been asked to design a room in a dolls house but using only recyclable materials. Mrs Mentary loved the beautiful museum containing children's toys and games past and present.

Each artist had been given a small stand to set up their dolls house room in a special exhibitions area in the museum. Mrs Mentary was there to watch the set up before the exhibition opened the next day. She went in and met some of the staff and the exhibitors. The curator in charge of the exhibition was Matthew Orles, a vibrant fifty-something in a multi-coloured jump suit. He had two assistants with him, Rob W. Whaf, an efficient young man who knew everyone's name and Karly Hol who by contrast seemed rather scatty and disorganised.

Matthew introduced Mrs Mentary to the exhibitors who had used a variety of plastic bottles, driftwood, used fishing nets, discarded clothes and electric equipment. The following contributors had created miniature bedrooms; Nat Temp, a sculptor who had exhibited at the Royal Academy, Sarah Ingrids, a Welsh woman who carved love spoons and Sally Letterman, a carpenter who made cabinet jewellery boxes. The following people had created small kitchens complete with cooking pans and utensils and yummy looking plates of fruits and vegetables; Lee Juby, a goldsmith from Cornwall, Robert Rought, a mechanical music box maker, Venetia Rouse who made old fashioned style china dolls and Antony V. Dell, a puppet-maker.

Next, Mrs Mentary viewed the miniature dining rooms complete with tables, chairs, dressers and dinner services made by Rolf Doldock who specialised in miniature paintings, Rabi Anar who normally made teddy bears and Vinay Parjeet, a woodcarver. There was one competitor, Eleanor Grimes, a ceramicist, that had created a whole bathroom complete with a working flush toilet made using old fishing line. Finally there were three lovely drawing rooms in a variety of period styles created by Victory Andalbert, a pop artist who had created a retro sixties room, Reg Nart, a textile designer who had created a Regency room fit for Elizabeth Bennett and Rose N. Deat, an upholsterer, who had created a futuristic space-age room complete with gold metallic fabrics.

Mrs Mentary loved the stunning details of the creations and was blown away by the quality of the craftsmanship. Once all the guests had had a chance to admire the exhibits, the competitors were taken into another room for a quick question and answer session with the press. It became apparent that although the creations were exquisite, there was not a lot of love lost between the exhibitors. Mrs Mentary was about to go home when everyone heard a huge crash from the room containing the exhibits. Everyone rang in to see Eleanor's beautiful bathroom smashed to pieces on the floor. Who could have done this awful thing? Help Mrs Mentary find the perpetrator of this dreadful crime!

———ele———

1. Matthew Orles – Innocent/Guilty, 2. Rob W. Whaf – Innocent/Guilty, 3. Karly Hol – Innocent/Guilty, 4. Nat Temp – Innocent/Guilty, 5. Sarah Ingrids – Innocent/Guilty, 6. Sally Letterman – Innocent/Guilty, 7. Lee Juby – Innocent/Guilty, 8. Robert Rought – Innocent/Guilty, 9. Venetia Rouse– Innocent/Guilty, 10. Antony V. Dell – Innocent/Guilty, 11. Rolf Doldock – Innocent/Guilty, 12. Rabi Anar – Innocent/Guilty, 13. Vinay Parjeet – Innocent/Guilty, 14. Victory Andalbert – Innocent/Guilty, 15. Reg Nart – Innocent/Guilty, 16. Rose N. Deat – Innocent/Guilty.

———ele———

The Mystery Tour

Your trail starts at Bethnal Green underground station (E2 0ET) which is on the Central Line (www.tfl.gov.uk). Exit following signs to the Museum of Childhood.

Clue 1

Enter the gardens on the right. You'll have to be on *fire within* and as cunning as a *fox* to find the culprit.

Clue 2

Leave the gardens the way you entered and continue walking up Cambridge Heath Road towards Old Ford Road. Time to find your *inner child* and eliminate another suspect.

Clue 3

Turn right into Old Ford Road. It's time to *exercise* that brain so you are *fit* for the quest - it will stop you getting *confused*.

Clue 4

Is this quest as good as ones from *prior years*? *Initial*ly walk along Old Ford Road. It's important not to make any *assumption*s and follow the clues *to the letter*.

Clue 5

Walk up Approach Road and enter Victoria Park. Is is time to go for *walkies*? Perhaps a *lady* can help remove the next suspect?

Clue 6

Walk across the park and turn right onto Gore Road and then left onto Lauriston Road. What's that on the pavement to walk *around*? You'll need the *fountain* of knowledge to work it out.

Clue 7

You may want to have a look at the lovely shops and restaurants around Lauriston Road before re*start*ing the search. When you have done so you are looking for a *hero within*.

Clue 8

*Initial*ly, walk up to Grove Road with the park on the right. Is this the *gateway* to solving the crime? Will *victory* be immed*ia*te?

Clue 9

Leave the park, cross over the canal and walk down Grove Road. It's time to *take this* for your *great performance* (or alternatively use it to *take a shot*). Just make sure you're not *out of order*.

Clue 10

Retrace your steps and take the canal path. You are following the canal keeping Victoria Park on your right along Pavers Way. Walk along until you reach a T-junction at which you walk under Old Ford Road keeping alongside the canal and the park.

Is this the *key* to this *old* case or will it remain *lock*ed as you're so *mixed up*?

Clue 11

Continue along the tow path. *Initial*ly, you thought this quest was a right *royal* saga and a *bridge* too far!

Clue 12

Sometimes you need to stay *ground*ed and do it your *way*, even if you feel a bit new and *green*.

Clue 13

You are *enter*ing the final part of the quest. You've been a *tower* of strength and a *hero fit for Shakespeare*! Just don't get *mixed up* now!

Clue 14

Continue walking alongside the canal until you come to the next bridge. Just be careful of the bikes that tend to ride in the *middle* of the tow path here and sometimes knock your *arms* and legs! Climb up the steps to the street and turn left. This is the road that takes you back go Bethnal Green Station and you're *within* the proper *East* End. Walk down towards Bishops Way.

Clue 15

Continue back towards Bethnal Green Station looking initially for an impressive building fit for a *patriot*. The *committee i*s out as to whether you *may* find the culprit or not! Just keep *build*ing on your previous success *stone* by stone. Just follow the rules *to the letter* and this will be your best *year* ever!

If you continue down Cambridge Heath Road you will return to Bethnal Green Station.

ell

Where to eat, drink, shop and play

Victoria Park Village is a lovely place to browse the shops or grab a drink, meal or coffee. Bethnal Green and Cambridge Heath Road also have some good places to drink and eat.

Eating, Drinking and Shopping

The Solo Bistro and Cocktail Bar, Museum Gardens, E2 9PA (www.thesolo.co .uk) serves great cocktails and Italian food next to Bethnal Green Underground and Museum Gardens.

Gallery Café, St. Margaret's House Settlement, 21 Old Ford Road, E2 9PL (w ww.stmargaretshouse.org.uk) is a vegan café offering great breakfasts and lunches and a good calendar of events.

The Approach Tavern, 47 Approach Road, E2 9LY (www.theapproachtavern. co.uk) is a welcoming pub with real ales, great roasts log fires and a beer garden near the park.

Chambers Restaurant, 132 Lauriston Rd, Victoria Park Road, E9 7LH (www.t hechambersrestaurant.co.uk) is a Mediterranean restaurant with a rustic interior and outside terrace serving lovely dishes such as pizzas, pastas and meze.

The Empress, 130 Lauriston Road, E9 7LH (www.empresse9.co.uk) is a great gastro pub with warm traditional interiors which uses ingredients from local suppliers.

Pophams Bakery, 110a Lauriston Road, E9 7HA (www.pophamsbakery.com) is a really lovely bakery with amazing coffee, sweet and savoury pastries and fabulous toasties.

Bruno, 211a Victoria Park Road, E9 7JN (www.bruno-london.com) is a cosy and vibrant wine bar and bottle shop with indoor and outdoor seating.

My Neighbours the Dumplings, 178-180 Victoria Park Road, E9 7HD (www. myneighboursthedumplings.com) is a really cool dim sum restaurant and Asian deli.

Pavilion Café, Victoria Park, Old Ford Road., E9 7DE (www.pavilionbread.com) serves organic breakfasts, lunch specials and sandwiches next to the lake in the park.

Mexican Seoul, Bow Wharf, 221 Grove Road, E3 5SN (www.mexicanseoul.co. uk) is a Mexican-Korean fusion restaurant with a street food vibe.

Satan's Whiskers, Satan's Whiskers, 343 Cambridge Heath Road, E2 9RA (www.satanswhiskers.com) is a cocktail bar with a quirky interior focusing on taxidermy.

Shops

Bottle Apostle, 95 Lauriston Road, E9 7HJ (www.bottleapostle.com) sells wine and craft beers and ciders and has tasting sessions.

Ginger Pig, 99 Lauriston Road, E9 7HJ (www.thegingerpig.co.uk) is a farm-to-plate butchers offering great cuts of meat, game, pies and sausage rolls.

What Mother Made, 93 Lauriston Road, E9 7HJ (www.whatmothermade.co.u k) is a lovely shop selling gifts and children's clothes.

The Toybox (Facebook page), 223 Victoria Park Road, E9 7HD is treasure trove of toys and games for all of the family.

Sublime, 225 Victoria Park Road, E9 7HD (www.sublimeshop.co.uk) stocks ladies' and men's fashions and accessories. Stylish but affordable.

Branch on the Park, 227 Victoria Park Road, E9 7HD (www.branchonthepark.c o.uk) is a jewellers with fantastic gold and gemstone jewellery in stunning designs.

Playing

Victoria Park (www.towerhamlets.gov.uk) is London's largest and oldest public park, covering 86 hectares. It offers a range of community activities, events and live music. It hosts a pop up street food market on Sundays (www.victoriapark market.com). The Regents Canal borders one side of the park and there is great walking in the direction of Columbia Road and Broadway Market to the west and Hackney Wick and Stratford to the east.

Young V&A Museum of Childhood, Cambridge Heath Rd, Bethnal Green, E2 9PA (www.vam.ac.uk) is a lovely free museum celebrating the history of children's toys and clothes with lots of interactive exhibits and regular events. Great fun for even the biggest child!

Backyard Comedy Club, 231 Cambridge Heath Rd, E2 0EL (www.backyardc omedyclub.co.uk) is a fantastic venue for stand up comedy and cabaret where Jo Brand, Harry Hill and Dara O'Brien have all performed.

York Hall, 5 Old Ford Rd., E2 9PJ (www.be-well.org.uk) is a beautiful old 1920s building housing a multi-purpose indoor arena and leisure centre but is also an international boxing venue.

Tour Two - Blackheath
Trapeze and Treachery

B lackheath is a lovely village in South East London near Greenwich with a huge green and fine period terraces. Mrs Mentary always enjoyed a visit to this picturesque neighbourhood and was pleased to be covering the visit from "The Great Earl's Circus" one chilly February evening. As Mrs Mentary arrived she could see the bright red and yellow big top on the large green. She was here for the dress rehearsal before the first show that evening.

When Mrs Mentary entered the tent she could hear the voice of Earl Dartmouth, a burly American with a dark curly beard.

"I've changed the order so that Marielle is top billing and has two extra slots," he boomed.

"That means Lincoln, Philip and Nel, you will go second and not do the finale," he said to three wiry acrobats dressed in pink and green that had faces like thunder.

Mrs Mentary gathered that Marielle, a stunning blonde trapeze artist, was Earl's fourth wife and Earl was smitten.

"Terry, Ross and Meridie," Earl continued, pointing to three clowns wearing large clown feet and painted faces, "I've cut your slot by five minutes".

"Mary and Russel, I'd like you to cut out the fire breathing part of your act!" Earl shouted at a middle aged couple on roller skates.

"Rosalind and Georgiana, please remove three outfits from the quick-change act!" Earl cried pointing at two ladies in sparkly dresses.

"Del, Clare and Rupert, we'll need to cut out the knife throwing part of your act," he said to three jugglers wearing neon outfits.

"Earl, this is an ensemble circus, not a one woman show!" yelled Clare.

"Finally, Grace and Niall, I am afraid we will need to cut Woof Woof and Tiddles' act entirely since we need someone on the box office given its opening night," he said to an elderly couple who were with a Great Dane and a Chihuahua.

Understandably there was uproar from the performers about this. Mrs Mentary decided it might be best to make a discreet exit and return for the show later that evening. When she returned she was surprised not to see Grace and Niall in the box office. When she asked what had happened she was told that Marielle had had a bad fall in rehearsal because the trapeze rope had snapped. She had broken her leg and the original running order was back on.

When Mrs Mentary looked at the rope it was sabotaged! Who had done this treacherous deed? It is up to you to find the culprit!

—ele—

The Suspects

1. Earl Dartmouth – Innocent/Guilty, 2. Lincoln Kentchurch – Innocent/Guilty, 3. Philip Chesterfield – Innocent/Guilty, 4. Nel Abor – Innocent/Guilty, 5. Terry Voles – Innocent/Guilty, 6. Ross Clark James – Innocent/Guilty, 7. Meridie Priman – Innocent/Guilty, 8. Mary Rebecca Armitage – Innocent/Guilty, 9. Russel Ociavy – Innocent/Guilty, 10. Rosalind French – Innocent/Guilty, 11. Georgiana Royale – Innocent/Guilty, 12. Del Aboles – Innocent/Guilty, 13. Clare N. Hoonteld – Innocent/Guilty, 14. Rupert Hammond-Edgar – Innocent/Guilty, 15. Grace Usma Jesty – Innocent/Guilty, 16. Niall Tass – Innocent/Guilty.

—ele—

The Mystery Tour

Your trail starts at Blackheath Station, Tranquil Vale, SE3 9LE which is served by South Eastern (www.southeasternrailway.co.uk) and Thameslink trains (www.thameslinkrailway.com) (trains to and from London Victoria, London Charing Cross and London Cannon Street serving South East London). There is also a good bus service from North Greenwich which is on the Jubilee Line (www.tfl.gov.uk).

Clue 1

Follow the instructions *to the letter*. Walk out of the station and *initial*ly turn left up Tranquil Vale. You need to get *established* on this quest and make sure you *rebuild* your resources to *date*.

Clue 2

Continue along Tranquil Vale. Time to get some *refreshment*. Perhaps some words from *1897* can *inspire* the name of the next innocent party?

Clue 3

Time to *pray* for help in this convenient location so that you don't get *confused*.

Clue 4

Continue *to seek godly inspiration*. Perhaps a *four-leaved clover* will help find the next innocent person so you can move onto the *fifth* clue?

Clue 5

Retrace your steps and turn right into Tranquil Place and turn left into Lloyds Place and then Grote's Buildings. You're feeling a little *blue* about the search but it's time to be a *pioneer* and to not get *mixed up*.

Clue 6

*Initial*ly walk onto Hare and Billet Road. You're seeing *red* now so it is time to think outside of the *box* but still follow the clues to the *letter*.

Clue 7

Walk down Elliot's Place. You feel as *cold* as the *North Pole* in relation to solving some of these clues!

Clue 8

Continue down Eliot Vale just past Baizdon Road. A *date* could help you find the next suspect as long as you follow this clue *to the letter*.

Clue 9

Retrace your steps slightly and walk up Orchard Road and cross over the common and A2 to make *forth* to General Wolfe Road. Make sure you don't get in a *state man* and get the *right* answer.

Clue 10

Walk up Chesterfield Walk but not for *long*. Time to ensure your att*itude* is right and you don't get *confused*.

Clue 11

Turn left onto Charlton Way and walk along to Duke Humphrey Road. Don't be a *rebel within* and keep *march*ing.

Clue 12

Cross over the A2 and walk across the *field ignoring* any passing *donkeys*. Are you going around in *circles* with this quest?

Clue 13

March along the path to Prince of Wales Pond *initial*ly crossing Prince Charles Road. You're feeling *thirsty* again but are a *fountain* of knowledge.

Clue 14

Leave the pond - are there *fish within* there? Walk over to South Row. You need to solve this mystery quickly or it will be *night* time. It's important you don't *shield* yourself from the clues.

Clue 15

Walk down Montpelier Row. You're feeling like it is *time to rest your weary head* for a while since you're brain is feeling *scrambled*. Perhaps this establishment on the left can help and also remove another suspect and find the culprit?

Continue walking down Montpelier Row and you will reach Tranquil Vale. To get back to the station you turn left.

elle

Where to eat, drink, shop and play

The websites www.allthingsgreenwich.co.uk, www.visitgreenwich.org.uk and www.enjoyroyalgreenwich.org.uk provide great information on places to eat, drink and shop and things to do in Blackheath and around.

Eating and Drinking

Blackheath has a good selection of pubs, restaurants and cafés including some of the high-end chains like Pizza Express, Gail's and the Ivy Café. There is also a good selection of delis, butchers and grocers.

Zero Degrees, 29-31 Montpelier Vale, SE3 0TJ (www.zerodegrees.co.uk) has a great bar and outside terrace, restaurant and brewery on site. Cosmopolitan menu with a focus on classic Italian dishes like pizza and pasta.

Buenos Aires Café, 17 Royal Parade, SE3 0TL (www.buenosairescafe.co.uk) is an Argentinian restaurant serving steaks and grills, pizzas and pasta dishes and classic desserts based on family recipes.

Tziganos, 15-17 Monteplier Vale, SE3 0TA (www.tziganos.uk) serves Italian and Spanish inspired tapas in a rustic yet modern brick-exposed wall setting.

Le Bar a Vin, 72 Tranquil Vale, SE3 0BN (www.lebaravin.co.uk) offers over one hundred different wines from all over the world whilst focusing on France. There are French cheese and charcuterie boards along side French classics such as beef bourguignon or duck confit. The decoration is cosy and intimate, almost like being in a wine cellar.

The Hare and Billet, 1A Elliott Cottages, Hare & Billet Road, SE3 0QJ (www.hareandbillet.com) is a find old pub with a modern feel and good gastropub food right next to the heath.

The Railway, 16 Blackheath Village, Blackheath, London SE3 9LE (www.therailwayblackheath.co.uk) is right next to the station so perfect for an end of mystery tour drink! It has colourful modern interiors and serves pub classics with a gastro twist. There is a very good calendar of events and fantastic friendly vibe.

15grams, 30 Tranquil Vale, SE3 0AX (www.15grams.co.uk) is a small-batch coffee roastery serving great coffee and pastries with a focus on sustainability.

Shops

Blackheath has some top-end high street names such as Jojo Maman Bébé, Jigsaw, Oliver Bonas and COOK. It also has some great independent businesses.

Black Heath Books, 74 Tranquil Vale, SE3 0BW (www.blackheathbooks.co.uk) is a fantastic second hand bookshop overlooking the heath which also stocks other printed collectables such as maps, engravings and original film posters.

The Blackheath Bookshop, 34 Tranquil Vale, SE3 0AX (www.waterstones.com /bookshops/blackheath-bookshop), although owned by Waterstones still maintains that small, independent, community feel and stocks a variety of fiction and non-fiction books from new releases to classics.

Blackbird Boutique, 28 Blackheath Village, SE3 9SY (Facebook page) sells beautiful clothes and gifts with a focus on sustainability.

Lark, 30 Montpelier Vale, Blackheath, SE3 0TA (www.larklondon.com) is a fantastic shop selling fabulous gifts, homewares, accessories and clothes in a number of South London locations. I challenge you to come out empty-handed!

Blackheath Creatives, 16 Montpelier Vale, SE3 0TA (Facebook page) is a treasure trove of gorgeous vintage clothes, art, jewellery and homewares with a lovely café and great outside space for events such as comedy and music performances.

Postmark, 13 Blackheath Village, SE3 9LA (www.postmarkonline.co.uk) is a family-run, independent greeting card retailer with a number of stores in London. They have the ringing the best of British and internationally designed cards as well as a selection of gifts and stationery.

Mary's Living & Giving Shop for Save the Children, 10 Montpelier Vale, SE3 0TA (www.savethechildren.org.uk) takes great preloved items and presents them beautifully. There are some real treasures to be found.

Playing

The expansive heath is a wonderful place to walk, run or even do some yoga! There are regular events such as fairs and festivals held on the heath. The northern end joins the lovely Greenwich Park which is also stunning and has great views of central London from its mounds.

It is also only a short walk to the Royal Greenwich Museums (www.rmg.co.uk) of the National Maritime Museum, the wonderful 19th century clipper boat "The Cutty Sark", Queen's House and the Royal Observatory.

Ranger's House, Chesterfield Walk, London SE10 8QX (www.english-heritag
e.org.uk) is a Ranger's House is an elegant Georgian villa on the boundary of
Greenwich Park with a world-class art collection amassed by the 19th-century
businessman, Sir Julius Wernher. Over 700 works of art are displayed across a
dozen panelled rooms, and include medieval sculptures, ornate jewellery, Renais-
sance and old Dutch master paintings and French tapestries.

Blackheath Halls, 23 Lee Rd, Blackheath, SE3 9RQ (www.blackheathhalls.com)
is a performance venue offering music and theatre offerings through out the year.

Tour Three - Wandsworth
Evil and Easter Bunnies

W andsworth is a lovely leafy corner of London with fine Victorian and Edwardian housing surrounding a beautiful common close to the River Thames. It was a bright but cold day in March and Mrs Mentary was excited to be visiting to report on a local charity Easter bunny hunt taking place around the neighbourhood. Homeowners, shops and businesses were decorating Easter bunnies and hiding them in their gardens or windows. The event was being organised by Hilda Smithfield, the head of the Residents Association, and Mrs Mentary was attending a meeting organised by Hilda in All Saints Church.

When Mrs Mentary arrived you could have cut the tension with a knife. Hilda was criticising all of the bunnies that had been decorated by the residents. She had attacked Don Tram, a local tattoo artist, that his bunny was too "risqué". She had informed Rose Lansdown-Gordon, Ginger Bowlen and Holly-Jane Carlton, yummy mummies who wore designer lounge wear, that their bunnies were too dull and needed livening up. She turned next to Bert Hay, the landlord of the local pub, and said that his bunny was not family-appropriate given that it was holding a bottle of beer. At this point Bert swore and stormed out.

Next for her treatment were Sharon Inghams, a stout woman who ran the local bakery, who was told her hot cross bun eating bunny was not encouraging healthy eating and Ivan Chord, the head of the local school, whose bunny had been decorated by the Reception Class. He was told that the school's bunny was too "amateur". The local MP, Willem Thind, had painted his bunny in the colours of his political party and was told by Hilda that the event was intended to be politically neutral and he should therefore stick to the colour brown.

Bill Iard, Bobby Quinn and Jessica Quarry, who ran the local football club, tennis club and rowing club, respectively, were told that their bunnies were too "sporty" and would offend the elderly and infirm. The bright pink bunny created by the owner of the local nursery, Bryony Smart, was apparently too "garish" and the minimalist bunny designed by the local interior designer, Gina Lhom, was "not eye-catching enough". Three local art students, Alonso Tutton, Shar Buryman and Lea Vesper, produced their "bunny" which was three bunnies cut into pieces and reconstructed to make some sort of monster with six ears and twelve legs. Hilda's eyes almost popped out of their sockets.

Mrs Mentary loved all of the bunnies and couldn't wait to participate in the hunt. However, one person wasn't fit to join in the next day, Hilda. She had slipped over some oil that had been left on her doorstep and was in bed with a broken hip. Mrs Mentary sensed foul play was at work. Find the clues and help Mrs Mentary discover the culprit!

ell

The Suspects

1. Don Tram – Innocent/Guilty, 2. Rose Landsdown-Gordon – Innocent/Guilty, 3. Ginger Bowlen – Innocent/Guilty, 4. Holly-Jane Carlton – Innocent/Guilty, 5. Bert Hay – Innocent/Guilty, 6. Sharon Inghams – Innocent/Guilty, 7. Ivan Chord – Innocent/Guilty, 8. Willem Thind – Innocent/Guilty, 9. Bill Iard – Innocent/Guilty, 10. Bobby Quinn – Innocent/Guilty, 11. Jessica Quarry – Innocent/Guilty, 12. Bryony Smart – Innocent/Guilty, 13. Gina Lhom – Innocent/Guilty, 14. Alonso Tutton - Innocent/Guilty, 15.Shar Buryman – Innocent/Guilty, 16. Lea Vesper – Innocent/Guilty.

ell

The Mystery Tour

Your mystery tour starts at Wandsworth Town Station, 20 Smugglers Way, SW18 1EG which is served by South Western Trains (www.southwesternrailway.com) from London Waterloo Station.

Clue 1

*Initial*ly, leave the station and turn right onto Old York Road past the *terrace* houses. A *palindrome date* can help you find the first suspect to remove.

Clue 2

Leave Old York Road turning left onto Tonsley Hill. Turn left into Tonsley Place and then right so you are *within* Fullerton Road. Look out for some *decoration* that these houses have in common.

Clue 3

Continue down Fullerton Road looking for a *named trio*. Hopefully this tour is not driving you around the *bend*.

Clue 4

It's *time* to turn right onto Alma Road and then walk up to the A205. Look out for *three fat ladies* that may help to find the *prize*. You're feeling a little *blue within*. Perhaps a *book* may help you feel bett*er*.

Clue 5

Crossover the A205 and walk down a *tuneful* road. Perhaps some *side streets* can help to find the next suspect as you walk up to Heathfield Road?

Clue 6

Wind yourself left down Wandsworth Common Westside and then take a path on the right to *sail* across the common and A214, Trinity Road. You are aiming for the junction with John Archer Way. Have a look around for for something that might help the *confusion*.

Clue 7

Walk up John Archer Way and admire the grand building before you. Time to *build* on your past success and take *owner*ship of this mystery tour.

Clue 8

Return to John Archer Way and walk into the common heading towards the café. I hear they *mix up* a good smoothie. Perhaps there is time to play a quick *game* that can help you remove another suspect.

Clue 9

Continue through the park taking the first path on the left which will lead you to the bridge over the railway. Then take the diagonal path to Bolingbroke Grove. Walk down Honeywell Road. Look *around* for a *named residence* that *could be in sunny Spain*.

Clue 10

Turn left into Northcote Road. There are lots of great shops and places to eat *within* this street so you may want to take a break from the tour.

You've been a *brick* on this tour and a gift from *heaven*. The first clues have set a good *foundation* for the rest of the tour so there will be less *stone*s ahead.

Clue 11

Continue walking down Northcote Road until you get back to Battersea Rise (A205). Are the *tables* turned? Just give it your *best shot* and proceed with *temperance*.

Clue 12

*Initial*ly, turn left onto Battersea Rise (A205) and then right onto Boutflower Road and head towards the *railway* line. It's time to *bridge* the gap in this search but make sure you follow the clues *to the letter*.

Clue 13

Boutflower Road now becomes Strath Terrace. *Initial*ly, turn left onto A3036 (St. John's Hill) and walk down the street looking for a fine *symmetrical building*. To date you've been a real *brick*. Just remember to keep following those clues *to the letter*!

Clue 14

There is a little walk now *within* this part of *Wandsworth* until the next clue. Turn right onto Harbut Road and then left onto Nantes Close. Turn right onto the A214 and then *transport* yourself over the roundabout to Jews Row where you will see some *garage*s.

Clue 15

Take a path on the left just before The Ship pub and walk with the river on your right. Take the next left through some apartment blocks. Do you feel *weighed down* or *secure* in the quest? A *large object* may *contain* the secret to removing the last culprit.

If you continue up to Smugglers Way and cross over the A217 to Old York Road you will return to Wandsworth Station.

Where to eat, drink, shop and play

Wandsworth has a lot of great places to eat and shop. Aside from the more mainstream eating and shopping venues in the Southside Shopping Centre such as H&M, Pandora, Next, Greggs and McDonalds there are three main areas for independents; "The Tonsleys" which is along Old York Road, the "Between the Commons" area of Northcote Road and along St. John's Hill. You'll find many of the well-known high-end high street chains on Northcote Road including Gail's bakery, SpaceNK, Whistles and Molton Brown.

Eating and Drinking

The Alma, 499 Old York Road, SW18 1TF (www.almawandsworth.com) is a traditional British pub with rooms serving pub classics with a twist.

East Hill, 21 Alma Road, SW18 1AA (www.theeasthill.co.uk) is a stylish gastropub with great British food.

The Bolingbroke, 174 Northcote Road, SW11 6RE (www.thebolingbroke.com) is a friendly neighbourhood gastropub which serves a great Sunday roast.

Northcote Records, 8-10 Northcote Road, SW11 1NT (www.northcoterecord s.com) is a trendy pub that serves pizza and has live music.

The Ship, 41 Jews Row, SW18 1TB (www.theship.co.uk) is an eighteenth century gastropub with a fantastic riverside terrace and outside bar.

Megan's, 539-541 Old York Road, SW18 1TG (www.megans.co.uk) is a gorgeous Mediterranean restaurant with fantastic brunches, lunches and dinners and a nice outside dining area. It also serves bottomless brunch with unlimited prosecco!

Konnigans, 344-346 Old York Road, SW18 1SS (www.konnigansrestaurant.c o.uk) serves excellent sharing and grazing platters in an attractive shabby-chic setting. It has great breakfasts as well.

Zia Lucia, 356 Old York Road, Sw18 1SS (www.zialucia.com) is a local pizza joint with amazing wood-fired pizzas.

Le Gothique, The Royal Victoria Patriotic Building, John Archer Way, SW18 3SX (www.legothique.co.uk) is a French restaurant and bar with a fantastic cloisters area in a magnificent old building.

KIBOU, 175 Northcote Road, SW11 6QF (www.kibou.co.uk) is a chic Japanese serving amazing food, cocktails and sake.

Red Setter, 32-38 Northcote Road, SW11 1NZ (www.urbanpubsandbars.com) is a great bar-restaurant offering everything from brunch to cocktails to Sunday roasts.

Rosa's Thai, 54 Northcote Road, SW11 1PA (www.rosathai.com) serves delicious Thai food in a relaxed setting.

VE Kitchen, 39 Northcote Road, SW11 1NJ (www.vekitchen.com) is a lovely vegan restaurant serving tasty food in a modern setting.

Taverna Trastevere, 112 St John's Hill Grove, SW11 2RD (www.tavernatrastevere.com) specialises in Italian dishes from Rome and has a lovely rustic interior.

Cheeky Chicos, 126 St John's Hill, SW11 1SL (www.cheekychicos.co.uk) is a funky Mexican restaurant with great small plates.

Little Frenchies, 354 Old York Road, SW18 1SS (www.littlefrenchiescafe.com) serves great coffee (in the cutest French bulldog cups..) and a fantastic all day brunch.

Press Café, 49 East Hill, SW18 2QE (Instagram) serves tasty shakes, coffees and baked goods in a funky interior.

The Skylark Café, Wandsworth Common, SW18 3RF (www.skylarkcafe.co.uk) is a great café in the middle of the common serving everything from great all day brunches to burgers to cakes.

Alma Café, 47 Northcote Road, SW11 1NJ (www.almacafe.co.uk) has delicious brunches, lunches, coffee and cakes.

Story Coffee, 115 St John's Hill, SW11 1SZ (www.storycoffee.co.uk) is a small but perfectly formed coffee house with amazing coffee and great baked goods.

Shops

Anthology Boutique, 511 Old York Road, SW18 1TF (Facebook page) sells gorgeous ladies clothes and accessories in beautiful colourful fabrics.

Iris Fashion, 143-145 Northcote Road, SW11 6PX (www.irisfashion.co.uk) sells beautiful stylish ladies clothes from By Iris and other selected brands. It has a fantastic collection of stunning items.

Mary's Living & Giving Shop for Save the Children, 531 Old York Road, SW18 1TG (www.savethechildren.org.uk) takes great preloved items and presents them beautifully. There are some real treasures to be found.

Trotters, 86 Northcote Road, SW11 6QN (www.trotters.co.uk) sells beautiful children's clothes.

QT Toys, 90 Northcote Road, SW11 6QN (www.qttoyslondon.com) is a fabulous family-owned toy shop.

Chalkboard, 60 Northcote Road, SW11 1PA (Facebook page) sells fantastic educational games, puzzles and toys for children.

Bayley and Sage, 509 Old York Road, SW18 1TF and 95 Northcote Road, SW11 6PL (www.bayley-sage.co.uk) is a gourmet food and wine store selling fantastic deli items.

Hamish Johnston, 48 Northcote Road, SW11 1PA (www.hamishjohnston.com) is a wonderful cheese shop.

Playing

Take a stroll by the river or on Wandsworth Common (www.wandsworth.gov. uk). Wandsworth Common has a playground, café, bowls and tennis as well as woods and lakes.

Enjoy the annual Wandsworth Fringe Festival (www.wandsworthfringe.com) which brings together hundreds of creative people in a programme of theatre, comedy, music and art.

Tour Four - Bermondsey Street, Maltby Street Market and Borough Market

A Foody Fiend

M rs Mentary had been asked to write an article on a new food tour around London Bridge focusing on Bermondsey High Street, Maltby Street Market and Borough Market. The area is full of lovely delis and restaurants, artisan food stalls and shops. It was a lovely warm sunny day in April and Mrs Mentary was looking forward to sampling some delicacies including spring lamb and fresh asparagus.

The tour was being run by Rock Shieldsmith, a food journalist who obviously had a lot of passion for their subject judging by their well-covered physique. There was a group of ladies from the Women's Institute attending; Emma E. Austin, who from her muscular forearms obviously did a lot of kneading, Abbie C. Bermond, who had a large basket ready to fill with scrumptious goodies, Charlene Wright, who had a notebook with her and was noting down everything Rock said and Grace Bonny, who from the dirt underneath her nails Mrs Mentary assumed was a keen kitchen gardener.

There was a group of eighteen year-olds and their teacher from a Prue Leith cooking school. The teacher, Stephen Henrys, looked a bit flustered with his rather rowdy students who were Simon Carterton, a broad-shouldered young man, Ria Dyn, a glamorous girl whose fake nails in Mrs Mentary's opinion must impede any type of chopping or mixing, Miles Onest, a man with frizzy long hair which Mrs Mentary very much hoped was contained in a hairnet inside the kitchen and Boyce Compass, who was rather morose looking and Mrs Mentary assumed may have chosen the course out of a lack of aptitude for anything else.

Two friends who were setting up a delicatessen in Milton Keynes and wanted some inspiration for products, suppliers and presentation were also on the tour. The first was Yolande Johnson, a warm, bubbly lady. The second was Ness Trus who was a serious looking woman who kept asking about prices and margins so Mrs Mentary assumed was the one with the business acumen.

Also joining were Rishi Oner, who ran a business catering private dinner parties was looking for potential supplier, Ron Partial who was a professional food photographer and was hoping to make some contacts and Gwen Le Tuwell, who ran a food hamper delivery company. Finally, there was Terry S. Henry who was a tax advisor but really loved food and eating in his spare time.

The tour was great fun as they stopped at various artisan bakeries, butchers, delis and restaurants sampling morsels of delectable food such as Easter hot cross buns at Bakers' Dozen and locally made salamis at Pierre's. Mrs Mentary felt quite stuffed at the end and ready to be served up on a golden platter herself. Everyone had had a wonderful time when Rock got a phone call from the owner of Bakers' Dozen in a rage. Someone had put castor oil into the bread dough ruining their loaves and preventing them from delivering on their hotel and restaurant orders. Who would want to sabotage Bakers' Dozen's business in this way? Help Mrs Mentary find the guilty party!

— ele —

The Suspects

1. Rock Shieldsmith – Innocent/Guilty, 2. Emma E. Austin – Innocent/Guilty, 3. Abbie C. Bermond – Innocent/Guilty, 4. Charlene Wright – Innocent/Guilty, 5. Grace Bonny – Innocent/Guilty, 6. Stephen Henrys – Innocent/Guilty, 7. Simon Carterton – Innocent/Guilty, 8. Ria Dyn – Innocent/Guilty, 9. Miles Onest – Innocent/Guilty, 10. Boyce Compass – Innocent/Guilty, 11.Yolande Johnson – Innocent/Guilty, 12. Ness Trus – Innocent/Guilty, 13. Rishi Oner – Innocent/Guilty, 14. Ron Partial – Innocent/Guilty, 15. Gwen Le Tuwell – Innocent/Guilty. 16. Terry S. Henry – Innocent/Guilty

— ele —

The Mystery Tour

Your trail starts at London Bridge Station which is served by both London Underground (Northern Line and Jubilee) (www.tfl.gov.uk) and Thameslink (www.thameslinkrailway.com), Southern (www.southernrailway.com) and South

East (www.southeasternrailway.co.uk) trains connecting with Kent, Sussex and Surrey. Exit the station onto St Thomas' Street and walk up to Bermondsey Street.

Clue 1

*Initial*ly, you *read* the introduction *to the letter* and to *date* you've been a real *brick*.

Clue 2

Continue up Bermondsey Street. This trail is *right* up your *alley* and it's time to *share* your knowledge. Have you accidentally ended up in *Wales*? Perhaps a *creative type* can *inspire* you?

Clue 3

Retrace your steps from the alley and continue up Bermondsey Street to Tanner Street Park. The gentleman who *shares* is everywhere around here! It's so *confusing*! Perhaps *his favourite material* can help reveal another innocent person.

Clue 4

Continue up Bermondsey Street and *notice* a place for some *divine* inspiration since you're getting *mixed up* all of the *time*. Perhaps a *relevant person* can help?

Clue 5

Turn left onto Long Lane. You're feeling a little *thirsty*. Perhaps this *nineteenth century gift* can help?

Clue 6

Cross over to Bermondsey Square. You're feeling a little *blue*. Perhaps some *religious* instruction is in *order*?

Clue 7

Cross over to St Mary Magdalen church yard opposite which is open to the *public*. Isn't this a *pretty* space? *May*be the *two church wardens* work together to keep it so *elegant*?

Clue 8

Turn left out of the church yard and walk down Tower Bridge Road and turn the *direction* right into Tanner Street. Perhaps this is the *gateway* to finding the next suspect?

Clue 9

*Initial*ly, you will see the entrance to Maltby Street Market on Rope Walk. Enter the market and enjoy the delicious food options! Make sure you get the right *days* in the *month* when the market is open. Take a left down Millstream Road to travel under the railway and then turn left to walk down Druid Street. There are more fabulous artisan bakeries, brewing companies and restaurants to *shelter* in here (plus a rather lovely Porsche garage!) and none of it costs a *bomb*. Just make sure you continue to follow the instructions *to the letter* and you'll have a wonderful time.

Clue 10

Cross over Tower Bridge Road and continue to walk down Druid Street and go *within* St John's Churchyard. They say the *beginning is sometimes the same as the end* (in all *languages*). That's the *name* of the game!

Clue 11

Walk down Crucifix Lane and turn left onto Snowfields until Kirby Grove. You pass a few pubs. Perhaps they have this *smooth draught within*. It's *namesake building* will help you remove another suspect.

Clue 12

You continue walking and the road becomes Newcomen Street. *Pass a few sporting roads* and look for a *spot* of *charity* that *sounds like* it could help solve this mystery.

Clue 13

Continue to Borough High Street and turn right. Take the left fork down Borough High Street. This quest is *flying* out of control. You need a *saviour* or a *saint* to help you *within*.

Clue 14

You're now within Borough Market. The market is open on certain days and you'll also find wonderful food shops, bars and restaurants in the streets and railway arches. Once you have had a wander go to the corner of Winchester Street and Cathedral Street. You've *weathered* the storm and been as strong as a *stone* even when things were *grave*.

Clue 15

Continue up Cathedral Street back to Borough High Street and cross over onto St Thomas Street walking back towards London Bridge Station. Come on *guys,* don't be a doubting *Thomas* and look so *blue.* You just need the right *chemist*ry to solve the mystery by removing the last suspect.

If you continue along St Thomas Street you will return to London Bridge Station.

ell

Where to eat, drink, shop and play

Foodies will be in their element in this gastro playground but there are also a lot of other shops and attractions to enjoy. Check out bermondseystreet.london, www.maltbystreetmarket.co.uk and boroughmarket.org.uk.

Eating and Drinking

Trivet, 36 Snowsfields, SE1 3SU (www.trivetrestaurant.co.uk) is the first solo restaurant from Jonny Lake and Isa Bal who both worked at the Fat Duck and has a Michelin star. Expect exquisite innovative food. potato in a dessert anyone?

José, 194 Bermondsey St, SE1 3TQ (www.josepizarro.com) is a wonderful walk-in only Spanish tapas restaurant with a counter/bar eating area – one of Mrs Mentary's favourites.

Casse-Croûte, 109 Bermondsey Street, SE1 3XB (www.cassecroute.co.uk) is a small French restaurant with an ever-changing menu and an intimate feel.

Café Murano, 184 Bermondsey Street, SE1 3TQ (www.cafemurano.co.uk) has an open kitchen serving Angela Hartnett's classic and modern Italian dishes for a chic counter-dining experience.

The Garrison, 99 – 101 Bermondsey Street, SE1 3XB (www.thegarrison.co.uk) is a fantastic gastropub with exposed walls and vintage interiors.

Poulet, 37 Maltby Street, SE1 3PA (www.poulet.biz) is a chicken rotisserie restaurant in the arches that also serves amazing cocktails. Funky interior.

Wright's Brothers, Stoney Street, SE1 9AD (www.thewrightbrothers.co.uk) serves the most delectable oysters as well as other seafood. Some tables but Mrs Mentary loves siting at the bar.

Roast, The Floral Hall, Stoney Street, SE1 1TL (www.roast-restaurant.com) serves wonderful roast dinners in a first floor conservatory overlooking Borough Market.

Camille, 2-3 Stoney Street, SE1 9AA (www.camillerestaurant.co.uk) serves French dishes with a long list of ever-changing specials on chalk boards in the lovely rustic yet sophisticated interior.

Akara, Arch 208, 108 Stoney Street, SE1 9AD (www.akaralondon.co.uk) serves amazing West African dishes like spatchcocked Lagos chicken, plantain and grilled octopus.

Kolae, 6 Park Street, SE1 9AB (www.kolae.com) serves fragrant and delicious Thai food in a former coach house.

40 Maltby Street, SE1 3PG (www.40maltbystreet.com) is a bistro style restaurant located in a wine shop in the arches.

Chapter 72, 72 Bermondsey Street, SE1 3UD (www.chapter-72.com) is a stylish coffee shop offering great coffee, baked goods and cocktails.

Watchhouse, 199 Bermondsey Street, SE1 3UW and 36 Maltby Street, SE1 3PA (www.watchhouse.com) are lovely cafés and coffee shops with great food and coffee. The former is set in a nineteenth century graveyard watch house and the latter is in the arches.

Crol and Co, 66A Newcomen Street, SE1 1YT and 9 Tanner Street, SE1 3LE (www.crolandcocoffee.com) serves fantastic coffee and baked goodies by day and cocktails, wine and beer in the evenings.

The Gentlemen Baristas, 11 Park Street, SE1 9AB (www.thegentlemenbarista s.com) serves great coffee and lovely sweet and savoury pastries in the edge of Borough Market.

Monmouth Coffee Company, 6 Park Street, SE1 9AB (www.monmouthcoffee.co.uk) serves amazing fair trade coffee, pastries and other treats as well as bags of coffee to take home.

Vinegar Yard, 72 to 82 St Thomas Street, SE1 3QX (www.vinegaryard.london) is a large space containing food, drink and art stalls with plenty of outside and inside areas to sit. It holds a weekly flea market. Great atmosphere.

Shops

B Street Deli, 88 Bermondsey Street, SE1 3UB (www.bstreetdeli.co.uk) is a great deli selling tasty treats including charcuterie, cheeses, breads and coffees.

Morocco Bound, 1A Morocco Street, SE1 3HB (www.moroccobound.co.uk) is a book shop, bar and events space.

Seaward & Stearn, 112 Bermondsey Street, SE1 3TX (www.seawardandstearn.com) sell stylish classic menswear with a modern twist.

Mary's Living & Giving Shop for Save the Children, 90 Bermondsey Street, SE1 3UB (www.savethechildren.org.uk) takes great preloved items and presents them beautifully – some real treasures to be found.

Estella Bartlett, 132a Bermondsey Street, SE1 3TX (www.estellabartlett.com) sells stunning but reasonable jewellery and accessories.

Alex Monroe, 37 Snowfields, SE1 3SU (www.alexmonroe.com) sells beautifully crafted and original jewellery - Mrs Mentary loves the rocket-shaped locket!

Bermondsey Antique Market, 11 Bermondsey Square, SE1 3UN (www.bermondseyantiquemarket.co.uk) is a Friday market selling antiques, vintage items and collectibles.

Bird and Blend Tea Company, 7 Park Street, SE1 9AB (www.birdandblendtea.com) is a tea mixology company with a focus on sustainability.

Neal's Yard Dairy, 8 Park Street, SE1 9AB (www.nealsyarddairy.co.uk) is a world famous cheese maker. Mrs Mentary loves looking at the huge rounds of cheeses in the windows!

The Ginger Pig, Borough Market, 122-124 Druid Street, SE1 2HH and Borough High Street, SE1 1TL (www.thegingerpig.co.uk) is a farm to plate butchers stocking all cuts of British meats as well as fantastic sausage rolls and pies.

Playing

White Cube Gallery, 144-152, Bermondsey St, SE1 3TQ (www.whitecube.com) is a stunning contemporary art gallery with very large exhibition spaces, a court-yard, auditorium and bookshop.

Fashion and Textile Museum, 83 Bermondsey St, SE1 3XF (www.fashiontextil emuseum.org) showcases contemporary textile design and fashion.

Bread Ahead, Borough Market, Cathedral St, SE1 9DE (www.breadahead.com) offers bakery and cooking courses for all skill levels.

The Shard Viewing Platform, 32 London Bridge St, SE1 9SG (www.the-shard.com) offers visitors amazing 360-degree views for up to 40 miles being the highest viewing platform in London.

Tower Bridge, Tower Bridge Rd, SE1 2UP (www.towerbridge.org.uk) can be explored inside as well as out with amazing walkways and glass floors offering spectacular views of the River Thames and London skyline.

Bridge Theatre, 3 Potters Fields, SE1 2SG (www.bridgetheatre.co.uk) is a nine hundred-seat modern theatre which focuses on the commissioning and produc-tion of new shows.

Tour Five - Barnes

Avian Artifice

It was a cool but bright April day and Mrs Mentary was visiting the leafy village of Barnes to cover a "bird bonanza" at the London Wetland Centre. A group of volunteer twitchers were doing a weekend marathon birdwatch to raise funds for the centre. Mrs Mentary was a big fan of Barnes with its lovely green spaces, riverside setting and fine period housing.

Mrs Mentary was greeted by Gordon Greenway, a tall lanky young man with limp hair. He enthusiastically showed her the makeshift hides that had been erected for the event and introduced her to the other birdwatchers.

In the first hide she met three lifelong friends who had gone on birdwatching trips together for forty-years, Val Tugthoss, Emilie D. Kramer and Rita Green-Hopkins. They perkily offered Mrs Mentary some hot tea from a flask and showed her their top of the range binoculars. Next, she met boyfriend and girlfriend, Marc Pew and Emma Newell, who looked like they may have been having a row from their somewhat frosty behaviour to each other. Further into the reserve she was introduced to two elderly men, Victor I. Acott and Seamus O'Connor, who had very weathered skin and were wearing battered camouflage gear. They pointed out some of the species of wetland birds to her and for the first time Mrs Mentary understood the fascination of studying our feathered friends.

Next, she was introduced to four teenagers, Talia R. Berns, Charles Rose, Samira Ebrahim and Rowe Saker, from the Young Ornithologists society who already had a huge passion for nature despite their young age. She was impressed with their knowledge, maturity and dedication. She wasn't sure if she would have been sitting out in all weathers studying birds at the age of fifteen!

There was a professional wildlife photographer, Kate Sudgen, who had travelled the world taking photos for publications such as National Geographic. She had been asked to record the event but also create five large photo billboards for the centre. She had some amazing equipment with her costing tens of thousands of pounds including lenses that wouldn't have been out of place with the paparazzi.

Bea Hyve, a short stocky fifty-something and Rose G. Houve, a glamorous woman who looked somewhat out of place in the wetlands, were there recording the event for LondonLoves radio station and GoLondon television show, respectively. She had a good chat with them about their journalistic backgrounds and they shared war stories.

Finally, a grandfather and granddaughter, Robert-Ian Illas and Breanne Serg, who were celebrating their seventieth and twenty-first birthdays, respectively, by participating in the event. Breanne explained how she had been visiting the centre since she was four with her grandfather and how he ignited her interest in nature.

Mrs Mentary was back at the centre HQ having a cup of hot tea and a chocolate biscuit when Kate came running in. One of her top-notch lenses costing over two thousand pounds had gone missing. Which villain had stolen the lens? It's up to you to find the clues in Barnes and help Mrs Mentary solve the crime!

—ℓℓ—

The Suspects

1. Gordon Greenway – Innocent/Guilty, 2. Val Tugthoss – Innocent/Guilty, 3. Emilie D. Kramer – Innocent/Guilty, 4. Rita Green-Hopkins – Innocent/Guilty, 5. Marc Pew – Innocent/Guilty, 6. Emma Newell – Innocent/Guilty, 7. Victor I. Acott – Innocent/Guilty, 8. Seamus O'Connor – Innocent/Guilty, 9. Talia R. Berns – Innocent/Guilty, 10. Charles Rose – Innocent/Guilty, 11. Samira Ebrahim – Innocent/Guilty, 12 Rowe Saker – Innocent/Guilty, 13. Bea Hyve – Innocent/Guilty, 14. Rose G. Houve – Innocent Guilty, 15. Robert-Ian Illas – Innocent/Guilty, 16. Breanne Serg – Innocent/Guilty.

The Mystery Tour

Your tour starts at Barnes station which is served by South Western Trains (www.southwesternrailway.com) from Waterloo.

Clue 1

*Initial*ly, take Station Road heading towards Barnes Green. You cannot turn *yellow* with fear and need to be a real *brick* on this tour. If you do this and follow the clues *to the letter* you'll have your best *year* yet and find your *prospect*.

Clue 2

Continue walking down Station Road to Brook-wood Avenue. You need to be a *tower* of resolution and as strong as a *lion* for this tour so you don't get *mixed up*. Does this photo help?

Clue 3

Continue on. This is a *baptis*m of fire so you need to be as tough as *stone*! Time to seek out a *husband and wife* who *together* can help eliminate the next suspect.

Clue 4

Time to be *open* and get in the *right space*. It will stop you feeling *confused* even if you are feeling a little *green* at solving mysteries.

Clue 5

*Initia*lly, walk *right* through the green heading for Grange Road. Make sure to *shield* yourself from any angry swans! Turn left onto Church Road. A *gateway to learning* could help you remove the next suspect.

Clue 6

*Initia*lly, continue walking down Church Road following the directions *to the letter*. Hopefully there is no im*pediment* to your progress this *year* or you'll feel like you are in the Bermuda *Triangle*.

Clue 7

Walk down Barnes High Street enjoying all of the shops and restaurants *across* the way. Walk to *the River Thames* so you can admire the *boat*s. Time to join the *club* of fantastic detectives!

Clue 8

*S*troll, *j*og or *w*alk down *The Terrace* heading to Barnes Bridge. You are looking *for* the next clue *within*.

Clue 9

Continue walking down The Terrace. You are starting to feel a bit *blue*. Just stay *compose*d and *r*emember *the planets* may get back *into order*.

Clue 10

*Initial*ly walk under Barnes *Bridge*. Isn't it *striking*? You think the culprit's days are *number*ed if you keep following these clues *to the letter* and keep on the *rail*s.

Clue 11

Walk along The Terrace *initial*ly noticing some buildings *tower*ing above you. Will you party like it's the *year* 1999 at the end of this tour? Only if you keep following the *instructions to the letter*.

Clue 12

Turn left into White Hart Lane enjoying more of the shops and restaurants *Barnes* has to offer. As you walk you wonder if this *trail is beneath you*? It's important not to *tread on* your dreams to find the villain and to ensure things don't get *topsy-turvy*.

Clue 13

This tour is as sweet as *honey*! Turn left onto Railway Side keeping the track and allotments on your right. I am sure that there are lots of *insects* and other wildlife there and it's *buzzing* with activity.

Clue 14

Cross over Cross Street and keep walking down Railway Side. *Sounds like* this tour is an over*arch*ing success and has been a real *window* into detective work.

Clue 15

Keep walking down Railway Side until you see the underpass at which point turn right and follow the path keeping Wine Road Recreation Ground on your right. Turn left onto Vine Road and carefully cross over the railway. You feel like you've covered a *large area* since the last clue. Hopefully you'll come up *smelling of*....and remove the last suspect and find the culprit!

To the right there is a path that follows the right hand edge of Barnes Common Cricket Ground which will take you back to Barnes Station.

ell

Where to eat, drink, shop and play

Barnes is a great place to hang out for the day with some beautiful places to eat, shop and take a stroll. The main areas are Station Road from Barnes Green to the River Thames, Church Road from Barnes Green to Castelnau and White Hart Lane from The Terrace to the railway. There are a lot of excellent dining venues in Barnes which is why the list below is extensive!

Eating and Drinking

Rick Stein, Tideaway Yard, 125 Mortlake High Street, SW14 8SW (www.rickstein.com) is a great seafood restaurant with amazing views of the Thames.

Church Road, 94 Church Road, SW13 9HR (www.churchroadsw13.co.uk) is a chic modern European restaurant with great food.

Ela & Dhani, 127 Church Road, SW13 9HR (www.eladhani.co.uk) is a stylish Indian with beautifully presented dishes.

Riva, 169 Church Road, SW13 9HR (www.riva.restaurant) is a very popular Italian restaurant with traditional cuisine.

The Red Lion, 2 Castelnau, SW13 9RU (www.red-lion-barnes.co.uk) is a large Victorian pub with fantastic pub-classic food like fish and chips and sticky toffee pudding, great decoration and a huge beer garden.

The Sun Inn, 7 Church Road, SW13 9HE (www.thesuninnbarnes.co.uk) is a relaxed gastropub in a great location by the green with a fantastic outside seating area.

Coach & Horses, 27 Barnes High Street, SW13 9LW (www.coachandhorsesbarnes.co.uk) is a friendly tavern with hearty pub food, cask ales and wines and a very nice outside seating area.

White Hart, The Terrace, SW13 0NR (www.whitehartbarnes.co.uk) is a beautifully decorated tavern overlooking the river with very good food and an amazing outside terrace.

The Waterman's Arms, 375 Lonsdale Road, SW13 9PY (www.watermansarms.co.uk) is a gorgeous pub and restaurant overlooking the river with excellent food using seasonal ingredients.

The Brown Dog, 28 Cross Street, SW13 0AP (www.thebrowndog.co.uk) may be tucked away down a side street but it is very popular for its great interiors, excellent food and dog and children-friendly approach.

Alma Café, 2-3 Rocks Lane, SW13 0DB (www.almacafe.co.uk) has delicious brunches, lunches, coffee and cakes.

Hermanos Columbian Coffee Roasters, 7 Barnes high Street, SW13 9LW (www.hermanoscoffeeroasters.com) serves amazing coffee and baked goods.

The Nest, 56 Barnes High Street, SW13 9LF (www.nestcafebar.co.uk) is cute café with tasty and beautifully presented lunches and breakfasts by day and a cocktail bar by night.

Orange Pekoe, 3 White Hart Lane, SW13 0PX (www.orangepekoeteas.com) is a gorgeous tea room with loose teas for sale with a a nice patio seating area.

No. 40, 40 White Hart Lane, SW13 0PZ (Facebook page) is a lovely coffee, brunch and lunch café with some outside seating.

Cafe66, 66 White Hart Lane, SW13 0PZ (www.cafe66barnes.co.uk) is a café with coffee, food and baked goods including their own sourdough bread. It is a firm favourite with the locals.

Shops

Ridley London, 82 Church Road, SW13 0DQ (www.ridleylondon.com) sells stunning ladieswear in gorgeous fabrics and even has a service where you can choose certain styles in any fabric.

The Wos, 8-9 Barnes High Street, SW13 9LW (Facebook page) sells wonderful ladies fashion, gifts and homewares.

Dilli Grey, 23 Barnes High Street, SW13 9LW (www.dilligrey.com) sells pretty dresses, tops and accessories in quality fabrics which are ethically sourced.

Schuberts Footwear, 72 Church Road, SW13 0DQ (www.schuberts-footwear.com) stocks a great selection of stylish European footwear for men, women and children.

Mary's Living & Giving Shop for Save the Children, 64 Church Road, SW13 0DQ (www.savethechildren.org.uk) takes great preloved items and presents them beautifully. There are some real treasures to be found.

Presents, 22 Barnes High Street, SW13 9LW (www.presentslondon.com) is a great shop selling gifts, cards and toys.

Barnes Bookshop, 98 Church Road, SW13 0DQ (www.barnesbookshop.com) is a fantastic bookshop which will order any book in print for next day pick up and hosts regular events.

Wild Bush, 77 Church Road, SW13 9HH (www.wildbush.co.uk) is an excellent dog groomers that also stocks dog accessories. They even serve great coffee!

Ginger Pig, 61 Church Road, SW13 9HH (www.thegingerpig.co.uk) is a farm-to-plate butchers offering great cuts of meat, game, pies and sausage rolls.

Two Peas in a Pod, 85 Church Road, SW13 9HH (Facebook page) is a lovely fruit, vegetable and health food shop.

Barnes Fish Shop, 18 Barnes High Street, SW13 9LW (www.barnesfishshop.com) is an excellent fishmonger with a fantastic selection of fish and seafood.

Playing

OSO Arts Centre, Barnes Green, SW13 0LF (www.osoarts.org.uk) is a performing arts venue staging theatre, music and comedy shows as well as exhibitions and workshops.

Olympic Studios, Church Road, SW13 9HL (www.olympicstudios.co.uk) is a beautiful old cinema with two screens, reclining seats and a stylish café-restaurant with an outside terrace.

London Wetland Centre, Queen Elizabeth Walk, SW13 9WT (www.wwt.org.uk) is a stunning wildlife reserve home to a variety of birds, insects and mammals. There is also a discovery zone, play area and café.

Try your hand at some pot throwing and pottery at Ceramics Classes London, 19A Barnes High Street, SW13 9LW (www.ceramicsclasseslondon.com).

Riverside Gallery and Framing, 36 Barnes High Street, SW13 9LP (www.riversidegallery.co.uk) holds regular art exhibitions.

Chiswick House and Gardens, Duke's Avenue, Chiswick, W4 2RP (www.chgt.org.uk) is a stunning eighteenth century house and gardens with a café a twenty-five minute walk away across the river.

Hogarth's House, Hogarth Lane, Great West Road, W4 2QN (www.hogarthshouse.org) is the eighteenth century home of satirist William Hogarth and is a thirty-minute walk across the river.

Tour Six - Clapham
The Poisonous Popstar

Mrs Mentary was pleased to be attending the "Wannabe Tribute Act Festival" on Clapham Common in June. She loved Clapham with its huge green common, magnificent terraced houses and trendy bars and restaurants. She was attending the sound check so she could meet some of the stars. She was shown around by Rodney Evans-Bowes, an aged rocker, who said that he missed out on joining the Rolling Stones by a hair-whisker.

He first of all introduced Mrs Mentary to Stan B. Dand, Francis John and Al Provid who were all part of the Simply Red tribute band, "Basically Red". Next up was the ex-public school boy, "Eton John", Roger Hunt-Clyde, who apart from the fancy glasses looked nothing like his namesake. Marie Thyme, aka Tina Toner, was next and was wearing a micro leather mini and a bad wig. Unfortunately, No Direction were down to four men (Greg I. Edvard, Ted Adib, Oli Takely and Glen A. Certara) with one of the members having a stinking cold (and by the red faces of the others it looked like it was doing the rounds).

"Ted Sheerhan", Lex Anderg, had obviously dyed his hair red judging from the black roots but had a good crack at "Shape of you" despite not being in very good shape himself. "Dolly Mixture", Grace Thuttol, had a large fake bosom and even larger blonde hair and was dressed in cowboy boots and a cowboy hat covered in sweets. "Lionel Poorie", Les Barr, certainly had the snake hip moves but, unfortunately, the vocals didn't make Mrs Mentary want to dance on the ceiling.

"Cher and Cher Alike" was a man in drag, Catt Let, who had the voice of Cher (but, unfortunately, not the looks). The headline act was "Luke Warm Play", Nat Sume, Iain Harris-Adams and Keith Rodneys, with Keith trying his best to look like a dour Chris Martin despite being about twenty years older. Mrs Mentary noticed that the other performers were not very friendly to Keith who had the biggest trailer by far.

Mrs Mentary loves a bit of cheese and was really looking forward to the concert.

She had her picnic and glow sticks all ready on the common that evening. However, as Keith took to the stage there was a massive bang as all of the electrical equipment exploded! It looked like Keith wasn't going to get his headline act. Someone had hacked at the wires. Who would have done such a thing? Help Mrs Mentary find out!

ele

The Suspects

1. Rodney Evans-Bowes – Innocent/Guilty, 2. Stan B. Dand – Innocent/Guilty, 3. Francis John – Innocent/Guilty, 4. Al Provid – Innocent/Guilty, 5. Roger Hunt-Clyde – Innocent/Guilty, 6. Marie Thyme – Innocent/Guilty, 7. Greg I. Edvard – Innocent/Guilty, 8. Ted Adib – Innocent/Guilty, 9. Oli Takely – Innocent/Guilty, 10. Glen A. Certara – Innocent/Guilty, 11. Lex Anderg – Innocent/Guilty, 12. Grace Thuttol – Innocent/Guilty, 13. Les Barr – Innocent/Guilty, 14. Catt Let – Innocent/Guilty, 15. Nat Sume – Innocent/Guilty. 16. Iain Harris-Adams – Innocent/Guilty.

ele

The Mystery Tour

Your trail starts at Clapham Common underground station which is on the Northern Line (www.tfl.gov.uk).

Clue 1

It's *time* to turn right out of the station so you are *present within* The Pavement heading away from the common. Will this mystery tour be a *mare* to solve?

Clue 2

Retrace your steps and head towards the common walking along The Pavement. You are feeling *mixed up* and think some *refreshment* could help *though* what's available is *not* necessarily for *human* consumption. Is there any *association* with the mystery that could release a *fountain* of knowledge?

Clue 3

Walk across to the common. You *generally* still feel a bit *parched* and hope this will *provide* relief. Is this a *gift* of a clue? Just exercise some *temperance within* the tour.

Clue 4

*Initial*ly, walk across the common heading for *Windmill* Drive enjoying the views of the Long Pond. Is this going to be a successful *year*? Only if you follow the instructions *to the letter* and make sure you *stay* on course.

Clue 5

Start walking across the common to Clapham North Side. Is that *music* you hear? Perhaps it will help put things *in order*.

Clue 6

Walk down Cedars Road. It's important to *stay compose*d to *perform* at your best.

Clue 7

Continue walking down Cedars Road and turn right onto Wandsworth Road. Turn right onto The Chase. Are the *writ*ten clues helping you get clos*er* to a solution? You'll be an *angel* if you find the perpetr*a*tor and solve the *confusion*.

Clue 8

Continue along Cedars Road. This is a *novel* experience! Going *far* is the l*east* of your expectations.

Clue 9

Continue along Cedars Road and turn left onto Clapham Common North Side. You need to be an *architect* of your own destiny and dig deep *within*.

Clue 10

Continue walking down Clapham Common North Side continuing to *play* the game. This tour is very *drama*tic but you need to *build* on past success *within*.

Clue 11

Walk into the old town. You're feeling *thirsty* again and see a familiar sight to get a *drink*. Can you think how to find the next innocent suspect *within* the list?

Clue 12

You're feeling *blue* again. As mentioned before you need to be the *architect* of your success. That's the only way you get to own a *Bentley*!

Clue 13

Sometimes you feel all at *sea* and this mystery tour feels like *fish*ing in the dark or being a *boat* without a rudder.

Clue 14

There are two Grafton Square streets so follow these instructions *to the lette*r. Take the one furthest away from the common. *Initial*ly, walk through the square and then walk down Belmont Road and turn right onto Belmont Close. Are there some *strange people* around here? Perhaps finding a *location to pray* may help since this has been a tough *year*.

Clue 15

*Initial*ly, continue down Stonehouse Street and turn *left* into Cresset Street then right into Prescott Place. You're looking for some *godly inspiration*. Perhaps a *saint* could help stop you going around in *circles*? Look *above*. Is this *the door* to success?

If you continue on you will reach Clapham High Street. Turn right and you will reach the station in due course.

—ℓℓℓ—

Where to eat, drink, shop and play

Clapham has some very good eating and shopping options. The area around Clapham Junction station has a number of well-known high street options such as Accessorize, TK Maxx and Pizza Express as well as independents on trendy Northcote Road which is covered in the Wandsworth chapter. Abbeville Village along Abbeville Road has some lovely local shopping and eating such as The Ginger Pig butchers, 55 Abbeville Road, S4 9JW (www.thegingerpig.co.uk), Life of Fish fishmongers, 50 Abbeville Road, SW4 9NF (lifeof.fish) and The Abbeville gastropub, 67-69 Abbeville Road, SW1 9JW (www.theabbeville.co.uk). Clapham High Street stretching north from Clapham Common station has all of the standard high street eateries like Nando's and Taco Bell. The Old Town area is a real gem for independent restaurants and bars and a fantastic brunch spot.

Eating and Drinking

Minnow, 21 The Pavement, SW4 0HY (www.minnowclapham.co.uk) is a modern European restaurant with a great al fresco terrace.

WC Wine & Charcuterie, Clapham South Side, SW4 7AA (www.wcbars.co.uk) is a bar serving wine, cocktails and meat and cheese boards in a former public toilet.

Lina Stores, 22 The Pavement, SW4 0HY (www.linastores.co.uk) is a sophisticated Italian overlooking the common.

Megan's, 55-57 The Pavement, SW4 0JQ (www.megans.co.uk) serves fantastic food in a chic but relaxed setting in the Old Town.

Willows, 11 The Polygon, SW4 0JG (www.willowsclapham.com) serves amazing food including brunch tapas.

1833, 34-36 Old Town, SW4 0LB (www.clapham1833.co.uk) is a popular restaurant and cocktail bar with great foods.

Trinity, 4 The Polygon, SW4 0JG (www.trinityrestaurant.co.uk) is a fine dining restaurant with a seasonal menu served in a chic monochrome interior.

Upstairs, 4 The Polygon, SW4 0JG (www.trinity-upstairs.co.uk) is the more casual sister of Trinity offering small plates.

The Pig's Head, 87 Rectory Grove, SW4 0DR (www.thepigshead.com) is a farm to fork gastropub with fantastic roasts.

The Sun, 47 Old Town, SW4 0JL (www.thesunclapham.co.uk) is a traditional pub in the Old Town serving good food, especially Sunday roasts.

The Windmill, Clapham Common South Side, SW4 9DE (www.windmillclapham.co.uk) is a stylish pub and hotel in the heart of the common.

Brew & Barrel, 36A Old Town, SW4 0LB (www.brewandbarrelsw4.com) is a brunch spot turned cocktail bar with great reviews.

The Little Orange, 16A Clapham Common South Side, SW4 7AB (www.thelittleorangedoor.co.uk) is the ultimate house party bar with amazing cocktails, food and bottomless brunch.

Havana Coco, 10 Clapham Common South Side, SW4 7AA (www.havanacoco.co.uk) is a brilliant Cuban-inspired cocktail bar.

Bobo & Wild, 18 Clapham Common South Side, SW4 7AB (www.boboandwild.co.uk) serves great coffee, breakfasts, lunches and cocktails.

Lane Eight Coffee, 6 The Pavement, SW4 0HY (www.laneeightcoffee.com) serves great coffee in a minimalist setting.

Brickwood Coffee & Bread, 16 Clapham Common South Side, SW4 7AB (www.brickwoodcafes.co.uk) serves fantastic coffee, breakfasts and lunches in a relaxed but stylist setting.

Nardulli, 29 The Pavement, SW4 0JE (www.nardulli.co.uk) is an amazing ice cream shop with divine flavours like coconut and cardamom.

Shops

Trude's, 10 The Pavement, SW4 0HY (www.trudes.co.uk) is gourmet grocers which also serves take away coffee.

Village Wholefoods, 9 The Pavement, SW4 0HY (Instagram) sells organic, fair trade foods, fruit and beg and smoothies.

M. Moen & Sons, 24 The Pavement, SW4 0JA (www.moen.co.uk) is a butchers selling free-range and organic meats and deli items.

Clapham Books, 26 The Pavement, SW4 0JA (www.claphambooks.com) is a lovely independent book shop with a great selection of titles.

ChocoLit, 14 Old Town, SW4 0JY (www.chocolit.co.uk) sells children's books and chocolate in a delightful setting.

Playing

Take a walk around Clapham Common (www.lambeth.gov.uk) which is one of London's largest public spaces containing ponds, woodlands, three cafés, two playgrounds, a paddling pool, skate park and a community garden.

Attend the fresh food market, Venn Street Market, that takes place on the common every Saturday (www.vennstreetmarket.co.uk).

Clapham Picturehouse, 76 Verin Street, SW4 0AT (www.picturehouses.com) is an independent cinema with a bar which shows both mainstream, classic and arthouse films.

Omnibus Theatre, 1 Clapham Common North Side, SW4 0LH (www.omnibus-clapham.org) is a theatre showing a variety of productions including new writing in a former library.

Studio Voltaire, 1A Nelsons Row, SW4 7JR (www.studiovoltaire.org) is an arts organisation hosting exhibitions, projects and collaborations. There is a shop and restaurant on site.

Tour Seven - Stratford and Hackney Wick

Treachery on the Track

I t was a balmy July day as Mrs Mentary arrived at the London Stadium, Queen Elizabeth Park in Stratford for a London Athletics meet. She was here to interview some of the younger athletes who were competing for the first time and hoping to be selected for the Olympics. The park was looking glorious with colourful flowers in the beds lining the canal and Mrs Mentary was impressed with the size of the stadium that was originally built for the 2012 London Olympics.

She was being shown around by Milli Onvo, an attractive young woman who had a slight limp. Milli had been a long distance runner but unfortunately a bad car accident had shattered not only her femur but her original ambitions to represent Great Britain in the Olympics. Nevertheless Milli enjoyed her new role working as an assistant for the athletes and was also training for the Paralympics. She introduced Mrs Mentary to Spence Tarr, a young man from Birmingham, who was competing in the 400 metres. He was quite quiet and looked like he wanted to just focus on his race. Mrs Mentary then met two young women, Mina T. Ionin with striking red curly hair and Posy-Sue Partraw with a blonde-bleached crop, who were competing in the long jump. They seemed to be the best of friends despite being competitors on the field. Mrs Mentary couldn't believe the distances they were able to jump.

Next, Milli introduced Mrs Mentary to two athletes who were competing in the shot put, Denise E. Avoning and Niel Sil. Their strength and determination was incredibly impressive and Mrs Mentary knew that the latter was seen as having a good chance of a gold medal. Sakura G. Itoshi was an incredibly tall and wiry 10,000 m runner who was enjoying their moment in the spotlight and happily chatted to Mrs Mentary about their ambitions. Richard Unwin-Newton, the 100 m sprinter, was less friendly and had a rather moody disposition. Mrs Mentary knew he had been suffering from injury and was nervous about the race.

Ben Otaf and Darell S. Slews were both competing in the high jump and there was certainly no love lost between them. They both glowered at each other at any opportunity. Corbi Thomas was a Welsh javelin thrower who was relatively new on the scene and had been touted as one to watch. Mrs Mentary chatted for some time to Lee-Alan Combe who had only just finished his A Levels and was competing in the 110 m hurdles. She was impressed with his eloquence and composure given he would be performing in such a large arena in front of thousands of people. August B. Edwards and Violette Amand were both competing in the discus and Mrs Mentary couldn't believe the width of their forearms. Ruth Erfor was a high hope for taking gold in the 800 m and was doing some meditation. She kindly agreed to take a break to have a chat with Mrs Mentary and Mrs Mentary admired her positive attitude. Damon Baxter was just grateful to be competing in the 200 m having got a spot because the other competitor had been injured. Finally Mrs Mentary met Lucy Bell, a mild-mannered Scot competing in the 400 m, who was just really pleased to be taking part.

Mrs Mentary was really looking forward to the event later that evening. As the crowd entered the arena the atmosphere was electric. The competitors all did well and some of them even attained personal bests. But where was Damon in the 200m? Unable to compete because he was down with a nasty bout of food poisoning. Everyone suspected foul play but who was the guilty party? Help Mrs Mentary find the culprit by solving the clues!

The Suspects

1. Milli Onvo – Innocent/Guilty, 2. Spence Tarr – Innocent/Guilty, 3. Mina T. Ionin – Innocent/Guilty, 4. Posy-Sue Partraw – Innocent/Guilty, 5. Denise E. Avoning – Innocent/Guilty, 6. Niel Sil – Innocent/Guilty, 7. Sakura G. Itoshi – Innocent/Guilty, 8. Richard Unwin-Newton – Innocent/Guilty, 9. Ben Otaf – Innocent/Guilty, 10. Darell S. Slews – Innocent/Guilty, 11. Corbi Thomas – Innocent/Guilty, 12. Lee-Alan Combe – Innocent/Guilty, 13. August B. Edwards – Innocent/Guilty, 14. Violette Amand – Innocent/Guilty, 15. Ruth Erfor – Innocent/Guilty. 16. Lucy Bell – Innocent/Guilty

The Mystery Tour

Your tour starts at Stratford station which is served by Greater Anglia trains to and from Chelmsford, Braintree, Colchester, Ipswich, Norwich and Southend (www.greateranglia.co.uk), the Elizabeth Line which connects Reading and Heathrow with Shenfield and Abbey Wood and Central and Jubilee underground trains (www.tfl.gov.uk).

Clue 1

Exit Stratford station in the direction of Great Eastern Road. Get ready for the *ride*! Just don't let off too much *steam* if you go off the *rails* and get mixed up. Don't *discount* the help you may get from *company* on the way.

Clue 2

*Initial*ly, take the pedestrian overpass that leads you into Westfield shopping centre. Walk through the shopping *centre* taking the path that takes you directly to the *London* Stadium, not Cherry Park Lane. Are things going *swimming*ly?

Clue 3

Are you doing *well* or is your mind *dancing* and getting *confused*?

Clue 4

Walk over Stratford Walk crossing the Waterworks River. Turn right and start looking around the park. You hope you'll be *cheer*ing at the end of the tour? Just listen to the *voice within*.

Clue 5

*Initial*ly, look across the river to spot a *cultural hub* which will give you a *sign*.

Clue 6

You need to stay *ground*ed *within* if you want to get the *gold*. Just don't make sure you don't *jump* to any conclusions.

Clue 7

Walk towards the bridge which will take you off the island to Marshgate Lane. You need to be as tough as *wood* to *work* your way to the solution. Just keep straight ahead on the *road* and you'll un*lock* the key and get things *in order*.

Clue 8

Head across the Diamond Bridge. Hopefully the answers to the clues will be *ring*ing *within* you.

Clue 9

Retrace your steps and head *for* Marshgate Lane. You need to be a *brick* and a *pillar* of *s*trength. What *qualities* will help you solve the tour and stay resolute *within*?

Clue 10

Once you have *read* this clue walk down Marsgate Lane and then head for Eastcross Bridge along Middlesex Way. Admire all of the *green* spaces *contained* in the park which will lift your spirit even if you are feeling *blue within*.

Clue 11

Retrace your steps and *initial*ly head for Waterden Road and the street and bridge directly in front of you taking you to Hackney Wick. Perhaps a *copper* can help find the culprit by thinking out of the *box*? But if they find him he'd better not...

Clue 12

Well done for solving Clue *11*!. If you continue down Copper Street you will find a bridge that takes you into Hackney Wick. This is a hugely vibrant area with lots of *men* and women enjoying the cafés and restaurants and whilst you explore and perhaps take some refreshment take a break from the tour so you feel be*tt*er. When you are ready to recommence head for White Post Lane and the bridge taking you over the canal. Once you have crossed the canal walk down to the tow path and walk along the canal admiring all of the bars overlooking it and canal boats. Take a left to walk back towards the London Stadium once you reach Stour Road Bridge. Walk across the bridge over the River Lee approximately *200 m* to the entrance to the stadium and turn right and start walking around the stadium on effectively a first floor walkway.

Have we found the *gate* to the solution – perhaps it could be *engraved* in your heart *within* if you let down your *barriers*? *Be* calm and you'll get at least a *silver*. Sometimes *who we are is what we achieve*!

Clue 13

Continue walking around the stadium searching for another *gate*way to *support* answers. *Do* make sure this quest does not go, go, go....and you keep everything *in order*.

Clue 14

Continue walking around the stadium until you get to the *large* bridge that takes you to Thornton Street. Keep being *structure*d and you won't be able to *contain* your joy when you find the culprit!

Clue 15

Sounds like you wish you'd studied criminology at *university* or *college* to assist with this *London*-based tour!

Once you've found the last suspect to remove and identified your culprit you can either turn right onto Pool Street to get to the Mountfitchet Road overpass which will take you back to Stratford Station or turn left to walk up and around the London Aquatic Centre towards Sadler's Wells to walk back through Westfield Shopping Centre.

Where to eat, drink, shop and play

There are a wealth of shopping and eating opportunities in Stratford. Westfield shopping centre, Montfitchet Road, E20 1EJ (www.westfield.com) has a plethora of high street shops including Sephora, Primark and John Lewis plus some high-end high street and designer shops such as Coach, Hugo Boss and Tag Heur. It also has lots of well-known food and restaurant chains such as The Real Greek,

Gordon Ramsay's Bread Kitchen and Café Nero. A great day can be spent in Westfield shopping centre browsing the shops and eating in the many restaurants which line the spacious boulevards but the below focuses on the independents you will find in the area.

Eating and Drinking

Barge East, River Lee, Sweetwater Mooring, White Pool Lane, E9 5EN (www.bargeeast.com) is a restaurant and bar on a floating barge. The food is seasonal, innovative and delicious. There are both inside and outside seating areas.

Cornerstone by Chef Tom Brown, 3 Prince Edward Road, E9 5NP (www.cornerstonehackney.com) is a clean-lined restaurant focusing on modern British cooking with exquisitely executed and presented dishes.

Burnt Umber Brasserie, 2 Hepscott Road, E9 5HB (www.burnt-umber.co.uk) is a contemporary European restaurant serving great brunches, lunches and dinners in a chic modern interior. It has lovely Sunday roasts.

Natura, 30 Felstead Street, E9 5LG (www.naturapizzeria.com) is a local Italian selling great pizzas, antipasti and pastas in a rustic yet modern setting. The vibe is cool and relaxed.

The Lord Napier Star, 25 White Post Lane, E9 5ER (www.lordnapierstar.co.uk) is a lively pub covered in bright graffiti-style murals offering seasonal food and good beer. It hosts regular events such as quizzes.

Hackney Bridge, Units 1-28 Echo Building, East Bay Lane, E15 2SJ (www.hackneybridge.org) is a bar, international street food court and events location with indoor and outside seating. It has an amazing vibe.

Grow, Main Yard, 98C Wallis Road, E9 5LN (www.growhackney.co.uk) is a warehouse space serving great coffee, breakfasts, lunches and suppers with a Middle Eastern, Mediterranean influence. There is regular live music and open mic sessions. It has a great location next to the canal.

Silo London, Unit 7, The White Building, E9 5EN (www.silolondon.com) is a white loft-apartment style zero-waste restaurant with a tasting menu. The food is stunning.

CRATE Brewery & Pizzeria, Unit 7 Queen's Yard, E9 5EN (www.cratebrewery.com) is a huge warehouse space with a outside terrace on the canal with its own micro-brewery with yummy original pizzas like sage and truffle and Middle Eastern lamb. There is a real party vibe with live DJ sets.

Beer Merchants Tap, 99 Wallis Road, E95LN (www.beermerchantstap.com) serves over six-hundred seasonable beers in a warehouse style space and courtyard.

There is a bar food focusing on cheese and charcuterie with burgers served in an outside shack.

Howling Hops Brewery and Tank Bar, Unit 9A, Queen's Yard, White Post Lane, E9 5EN (www.howlinghops.co.uk) has ten tanks of fresh craft beer in a warehouse style space and courtyard. Resident chefs serve a variety of international cuisine.

Rule Zero, 3 Succession Walk, Fish Island, E3 2RX (www.rulezero.co.uk) is a board game venue with great drinks, brunches, light bites, live music and a canal side setting.

Two More Years, 7 Roach Road, Fish Island, E3 2PA (www.twomoreyears.co.uk) is a graffiti-covered bar in an old warehouse with leather sofas, high ceilings and a canal-side location. It has DJ sets and a street food menu.

Thingy Café, 1 Trowbridge Road, E9 5LD (Facebook page) serves delicious breakfasts, brunches, lunches, coffee and cakes in an airy light-filled space.

Ethical Bean Company Coffee Shop, 41 Dace Road, E3 2NG (www.ethicalbean company.com) blend their own coffee but also provide a lovely friendly breakfast, brunch and lunch venue. They serve great smoothies as well as coffee.

Shops

Bad Coffee, 9 Oslo House, Prince Edward Road, E9 5LX (www.drinkbadcoffe e.com) is a roastery and espresso bar selling coffee blends both in their store and online. I love the fantastic bright yellow packaging! There is a small selection of baked goods to accompany the delicious coffee.

Refill Therapy, Unit 1 61-63 Wallis Road, E9 5LH (www.refilltherapy.co.uk) is a great refill shop with a really good selection of ethically sourced products.

Tuck Shop, 2 Casings Way, Fish Island, E3 2TH (www.tuck-shop.co.uk) is a grocer, butcher and bottle shop championing local suppliers and quality produce. They also sell take away coffee, bacon baps, sandwiches and pastries.

Wicked Bike Repair, Units 1-28 Echo Building, East Bay Lane, E15 2SJ (www. wickedbikerepair.com) rents, sells and repairs adult and children's bicycles. They have both new and refurbished stock.

Playing

Queen Elizabeth Park (www.queenelizabetholympicpark.co.uk) is a lovely space with different gardens and a waterside setting. There are various sculptures and information boards commemorating the London 2012 Olympics and good children's play areas. There are regular events held in the park. It's lovely to walk along the canal and see the colourful canal boats and locks and look up at the impressive stadium, orbital and other large structures in the area. There is massive investment being made in the area with new apartment blocks and events venues from big names like V&A and Saddler's Wells being built. It goes without saying that the area will continue to become even more exciting as these projects are completed.

Hackney Wick has a very trendy vibe and it's fun to simply stroll looking at the different bars and restaurants and soak up the atmosphere. The buildings are covered with graffiti art with some fantastic murals that make great Instagram opportunities.

Stratford East Theatre, Gerry Raffles Square, Theatre Square, E15 1BN (www.stratfordeast.com) is a Victorian theatre hosting excellent drama, music and comedy productions for all of the family.

Stratford East Picture House, Salway Road, E15 1BX (www.picturehouse.com) is a modern airy cinema which shows foreign, arthouse, classic and blockbuster films on four screens. There is an on site café.

The Yard Theatre, Unit 2a, Queen's Yard, E9 5EN (www.theyardtheatre.co.uk) is a 110-seat community theatre in a former warehouse showing theatre, music and dance productions.

Copper Box Arena, Copper Street, E20 3HB (copperboxarena.org.uk) not only offers gym and leisure facilities but is also an events venue hosting a variety of spectator sports such as basketball, wrestling and tennis.

London Aquatics Centre, E20 2ZQ (www.everyoneactive.com) is the former swimming and diving venue for London 2012 and has amazing pools, gyms and a restaurant on site café.

London Stadium, E20 2ST (www.london-stadium.com) is the stadium built for the London 2012 Olympics and is now the home of West Ham United FC. As well as hosting their home matches it also host regular events in both the sports and arts worlds.

Sadler's Wells East, 101 Carpenters Road, E20 2AR (www.sadlerswells.com) is due to open soon and will have a 550 seat theatre, studios, café, restaurant and publicly accessible dancefloor in the foyer.

V&A East Storehouse and V&E East Museum (www.vam.ac.uk) will be opening in 2025 and will open up V&A exhibits and events to a wider group of people as part of the Mayor of London's East Bank project. There will be an on site café.

ArcelorMittal Orbit, 5 Thornton Street, E20 2AD (www.arcelormittalorbit.com), being renovated at the time of writing (planned reopening 2025), is a tall sculpture built for the 2020 Olympic Games which offers amazing views of London and an enclosed slide.

Discover Children's Story Centre, 383-387 High Street, E15 4QZ (www.discov er.org.uk) is an immersive story-trail venue for children. There are lots of exhibits to interact with both inside and outside.

Tour Eight - Highbury and Cannonbury

A False Football Fan

The chants could be heard in full swing as Mrs Mentary arrived to cover the first game of the season at Arsenal Football Stadium in Highbury. Arsenal was playing Fulham and Mrs Mentary was joining fifteen fans that had booked a special experience to meet the players and have a backstage tour after the game. Everyone was incredibly excited to be meeting their heroes on the hallowed turf of the ground.

Mrs Mentary met the attendees in a hospitality suite. They were being looked after by an enthusiastic young man, William Johns, who was eagerly telling them about the plan for the day. Mrs Mentary met four young men who had been going to matches together since they were boys and were celebrating their twenty-first birthdays: Al Prid, Les W. Bowering. Joe Stiller and Ronald S. Francis. She met a well-rounded woman, Hannah Crowther, who had been bought the experience as a retirement gift after thirty-years working for the local council. Next, there was a very wealthy elderly American man, Thomas Henry, who was there with his glamorous but slightly bored-looking younger girlfriend, Roxy-Lee Ruhn. An eight-year old boy, Spenser Bacon, was being accompanied by his grandfather, Albert Bacon. Albert had brought a very old scrapbook containing autographs from players over sixty-years and Spenser was going to ask the Arsenal players to add their signatures to this.

Fred Hutchins was a local man whose recently deceased mother had worshipped Arsenal and he was here to pay tribute to her. There were three young women, Beth Kenn, Liv Edher and Rita Ges, who were very good footballers themselves and were on Liv's hen do. They were talking nine to the dozen in excitement at being there. Jane Wrivert was an elderly woman who had lived in the area all of her life and had not missed a single home game in that time. She was accompanied by her helper, a pretty red-head, Jan E. Wisman. Finally there was Rick Esto, a rich and portly city banker, who was spending a lot of time on his smart phone dealing with some urgent business matter.

Mrs Mentary watched the game with the other attendees. It was slightly disappointing with a 0-0 result but this didn't impact the guests excitement at meeting the players after the match. Mrs Mentary noticed that Roxy-Lee had slightly perked up now that there were some young, athletic men to flirt with. Spenser stepped forward with the scrapbook and asked the players to add their signatures. Albert took photos of his grandson and had tears in his eyes. After thirty minutes William took the guests to a hospitality suite where they had a lovely meal to close the event.

Everyone was about to leave having had an amazing time when Albert started to panic. His scrapbook had gone missing containing sixty years of memories. Who had stolen this precious gift? It is up to you to help Mrs Mentary find out by solving the clues!

The Suspects

1. William Johns – Innocent/Guilty, 2. Al Prid – Innocent/Guilty, 3. Les W. Bowering – Innocent/Guilty, 4. Joe Stiller – Innocent/Guilty, 5. Ronald S. Francis – Innocent/Guilty, 6. Hannah Crowther – Innocent/Guilty, 7. Thomas Henry – Innocent/Guilty, 8. Roxy-Lee Ruhn – Innocent/Guilty, 9. Spenser Bacon – Innocent/Guilty, 10. Fred Hutchins – Innocent/Guilty, 11. Beth Kenn – Innocent/Guilty, 12.Liv Edher – Innocent/Guilty, 13. Rita Ges – Innocent/Guilty, 14. Jane Wrivert – Innocent Guilty, 15. Jan E. Wisman – Innocent/Guilty, 16. Rick Esto – Innocent/Guilty.

The Mystery Tour

Your tour starts at Highbury and Islington station which is on the Victoria underground line and the Overground (www.tfl.gov.uk).

Clue 1

First, turn right out of the station and turn down the street with the *name* Upper Street. There are some good restaurants to be *found* here including noodle and *pasta* ones. Look for a *heavenly place.*

Clue 2

St*art* to walk down Compton Terrace and then turn left into Canonbury Lane to get to Canonbury Gardens. Turn down Canonbury Road. You need to be *creative* on this tour so you *collect* the clues effectively!

Clue 3

Start retracing your steps and take a look at *London's most beautiful square* (not at all *standard* whether it be morning or *evening*). Time to *build* on the success of previous clues but don't get *mixed up*!

Clue 4

By *George*, you're doing *well*! Not so *green within* now.

Clue 5

Walk over to Canonbury Place having left the gardens with their flowers and *herbs*. You are feeling a bit *blue* and *spen*t. Perhaps you can re*ce*ive a clue *within* here.

Clue 6

Walk down Alwyne Villas to the A1200 and take an immediate left as it *flows* into Canonbury Grove. It's time for a *novel walk around* this area.

Clue 7

Cross through the gardens to Willow Bridge Road admiring *the flowers*. Walk up Willow Bridge Road and then into Grange Grove. *Sounds like* you're doing well. Just make sure you keep waking up and *smelling the...*

Clue 8

Walk up St Paul's Road. Before you *cross* look out for something on a *house.* Will it help you be as *per*fect and as brave as a *lion within*?

Clue 9

It's *time* to walk up Highbury Grove to Highbury Hill. You need to be a *tower* of strength *within* to deal with whatever you are *presented* with.

Clue 10

Walk into Highbury Fields and continue walking unto you see the Baptist Church on the left and then walk up Highbury Terrace. You need to be *inventive* on this tour and your brain must work faster than *electricity*! Perhaps *tele*pathy will help (or a brain that can do photo*graphy*).

Clue 11

Walk down Ronalds Road. You should have *pride* in your performance. Be *loyal* to yourself since you've been the architect of your success. Just keep being strong like a *stone within*.

Clue 12

Walk down Battledean Road. Is there much *movement* in this tour? Just make sure you carefully follow the *print*ed word *within* the clues.

Clue 13

Direct or take yourself down Avon Road and turn right onto Drayton Park and walk up to Arsenal Stadium. Are you a *fan*? *Sounds like* this tour has required an *immense contribution* from you.

Clue 14

Retrace your steps and walk down Drayton Park and turn left into Holloway Road. Perhaps the answer is in a *book*. Just make sure you keep going so you are not on *borrowed* time. As they say it may *bring in the...*

Clue 15

Time to get some *divine inspiration* for the final clue or things will look *grave*. Make sure you stay squeaky *clean* and don't work yourself up into a *lather*.

If you retrace your steps and turn right onto Holloway Road you will return back to Highbury and Islington Station.

—e&e—

Where to eat, drink, shop and play

There are many amazing places to eat, drink, shop and visit in this area. The wonderful Upper Street that extends from Angel underground station, Islington to Highbury and Islington station is lined with fantastic cafés, restaurants and shops. There are also a number of streets in Highbury and Canonbury that have more local pubs and cafés.

Eating and Drinking

Trullo, 300-302 St. Paul's Road, N1 2LH (www.trullorestaurant.com) is a sophisticated Italian with excellent food.

Smokehouse, 63-69 Canonbury Road, N1 2DJ(www.smokehouseislington.co.uk) serves wonderful smoked and grilled food in a relaxed setting and has a great outside seating area.

Tootoomoo Islington, 278 St. Paul's Road, N1 2LH (www.tootoomoo.co.uk) is a chic pan-Asian restaurant with great dishes from Japan, Thailand and China.

Saltine, 11 Highbury Pak, N5 1QJ (www.saltine.co.uk) is a beautiful modern European restaurant specialising in sharing plates.

Zia Lucia, 157 Holloway Road, N78LX (www.zialucia.com) is a great local pizza joint with amazing wood-fired pizzas.

Brewhouse Kitchen, 24 Corsica Street, N6 1JJ (www.brewhouseandkitchen.com) is a modern pub with a warehouse feel, great indoor and outdoor areas and a relaxed vibe. It serves American feel-good food which includes burgers and steaks.

The Alwyne Castle, 83 St. Paul's Road, N1 2LY (www.thealwynecastleislington.co.uk) is a large pub with bright modern interiors and good seating inside and outside including within a conservatory. Hearty, satisfying food.

Canonbury Tavern, 21 Canonbury Place, N1 2NS (www.thecanonbury.co.uk) is a great gastropub with a wonderful beer garden in the heart of Canonbury. It has very good Sunday roasts.

Myddleton Arms, 52 Canonbury Road (www.myddletonarms.co.uk) is a traditional Victorian pub with great ales on tap and a grill menu.

The Highbury Barn Tavern, 26 Highbury Park, N5 2AB (www.thehighburybarnpub.co.uk) is an eighteenth century pub with modern interiors and hearty pub food, leather seating and open fires. It is known for its Sunday roasts.

Compton Arms, 4 Compton Avenue, N1 2XD (www.comptonarms.co.uk) is a small pub down a side street with covered courtyard serving beautiful Italian small plates.

Vagabond, 105 Holloway Road, N7 8LT (www.vagabond.london) is a coffee shop with an industrial feel which serves great breakfasts, lunches and baked goods.

EZ & Moss, 183 Holloway Road, N7 8LX (www.ezmoss.co.uk) is a vegetarian and vegan café which serves fantastic breakfasts, lunches and cakes.

Euphorium, 202 Upper Street, N1 1RQ (www.euphorium.uk.com) is a great café serving fantastic breakfasts, lunches, sandwiches and baked goods.

The Place, 11 Canonbury Place, N1 2NQ is a local café with a homely atmosphere and delicious food.

Profile Coffee, 16 Highbury Park, N5 1QJ (www.profilecoffeen5.co.uk) is lovely light and airy coffee shop with amazing coffee and fantastic food.

Highness Café and Tea Room, 21a Highbury Park, N5 1QJ (Facebook page) is a gorgeous café serving amazing baked goods and a delicious afternoon tea.

Udderlicious Ice Cream, 187 Upper Street, N1 1RQ (www.udderlicious.co.uk) is a wonderful ice cream shop with delicious yet innovative flavours.

Shops

La Peche Mignon, 6 Ronalds Road, N5 1XH (www.lepechemignon.co.uk) is a lovely French deli, patisserie and coffee shop with some indoor seating.

La Fromagerie, 30 Highbury Park, N5 2AA (www.lafromagerie.co.uk) is an artisan cheese shop with a great selection of British and international cheese.

Godfreys, 7 Highbury Park, N5 1QJ (www.godfreys.co) is a traditional butchers specialising in additive free and free range meats.

Provisions, 167 Holloway Road, N7 8LX (www.provisionslondon.co.uk) stocks a fantastic selection of cheese and wines and other deli items.

Monte's Delicatessen, 23 Canonbury Lane, N1 2AS (www.montesdeli.com) is a family-owned deli with a great selection focusing on Italian delicacies.

Maya Magal, 193 Upper Street, N1 1RQ (www.mayamagal.co.uk) sells beautiful hand-crafted jewellery as featured in Vogue.

Gill Wing, 182 Upper Street, N1 1RQ (www.gillwingjewellery.com) sells stunning contemporary jewellery including engagement rings with a focus on innovative design.

Cowling & Wilcox Ltd, 52 Holloway Road, N7 8BU (www.cowlingandwilcox.com) is an Aladdin's cave art supply shop.

Twentytwentyone, 274-275 Upper Street, N1 2UA (www.twentytwentyone.com) stocks contemporary and retro furniture plus homewares and lighting.

Aesop, 154 Upper Street, N1 1RA (www.aesop.com) has fantastic organic skincare products and home and body fragrances.

Mary's Living & Giving Shop for Save the Children, 138 Upper Street, N1 1QP (www.savethechildren.org.uk) takes great preloved items and presents them beautifully. There are some real treasures to be found.

Upper Street Bookshop, 42 Upper Street, N1 0PN (Facebook page) is a great independent book shop with a fantastic selection and knowledgeable staff.

Playing

Highbury Fields (www.islington.gov.uk) is a great place to stroll, run or picnic with a playground, tennis courts and café.

Walk the New River Walk (www.walkingbritain.co.uk) which is a scenic 1.5 mile stretch next to a channel of water in the heart of Canonbury.

Gillespie Park, 10 Tannington Terrace, Gillespie Park, N5 1LE (www.islington.gov.uk) is a peaceful park with ponds and walkways and an ecology centre.

Freightliners Farm, Sheringham Road, N7 8PF (www.freightlinersfarm.org.uk) is a lovely community farm with chickens, goats, cows and sheep.

The Hen & Chickens Theatre and Bar, 109 St. Paul's Road, N1 2NA (www.thehenandchickenstheatrebar.co.uk) is a small theatre above a fun and vibrant pub.

You can take a tour of Emirates Stadium visiting areas such as the players' dressing room and tunnel (arsenaldirect.arsenal.com). You can also visit the Arsenal museum.

Estorick Collection of Modern Italian Art, 39A Canonbury Square, N1 2AN (www.estorickcollection.com) hosts a collection of modern Italian art in a beautiful Georgian townhouse and also has an art library, bookshop and café.

Great theatre, comedy and music events are held at the Union Chapel, 19b Compton Terrace, N1 2UN (www.unionchapel.org.uk).

Almeida Theatre, Almeida Street, N1 1TA (www.almeida.co.uk) is a theatre hosting a fantastic range of exciting productions.

Everyman Cinema, 83 Upper Street, N1 0NP (www.everymancinema.com) is a turn of the twentieth century cinema with a retro feel, licensed bar and great range of new and classic films.

Tour Nine - Broadway Market and Hackney

A Market of Malice

I t was a sunny September day when Mrs Mentary arrived at Cambridge Heath Station in London's trendy East End and felt decidedly uncool compared with the young hipsters eating their smashed avocado and eggs and drinking their turmeric oatmeal-milk lattes in the railway arches restaurants. Mrs Mentary was here to visit Broadway Market and meet some of the stall holders in relation to a Eat East, a week-long celebration of East London's vibrant food scene.

Billy Blast, an Irish man who talked at one hundred million miles an hour, took it upon himself to show Mrs Mentary around. Billy sold savoury pies in all sorts of flavours and being one of the longest serving traders had the best pitch. Billy introduced Mrs Mentary to Ginny-Flossi Brast, a young woman with a plummy accent, who made amazing steak sandwiches. Mrs Mentary noticed a frostiness from Ginny to Billy. The next people that Mrs Mentary met were Leonard Oroe and Mona T. Ductant who ran a cupcake stall together. Their cupcakes came in delicious flavours and were exquisite to look at. Hanna-Kelly Wotch had a stall which sold Italian delicacies such as salamis, mozzarella and olives. Mrs Mentary couldn't resist trying some fresh burrata. Samuel Allen and Gerald Anderson were Scottish and specialised in the finest smoked fish and meats including smoked salmon cured in malt whisky. Liam Ham had a burritos and tacos stall and sold zero-alcohol margaritas which were delicious. What was interesting about all of the stallholders Mrs Mentary had met so far was that none of them addressed Billy, only Mrs Mentary.

Billy introduced Mrs Mentary to Dwaine R. Scour who made home-made lemon, lime and orangeade. Mrs Mentary could hear him mumbling something unpleasant about Billy under his breath. Quentin Jackson and Ruth Edoven made artisan breads and pasties and the smell was amazing. Lucia Borghoni was selling oils, vinegars and dressings and Mrs Mentary couldn't help but dip some of the available crackers into these and have a taste. Cat Tletro was selling home made ice cream in some really interesting flavours such as lavender and honey and Turkish delight. Mrs Mentary made a mental note to return later to buy a cone. Billy then walked over to a young couple, Ron Diseth and Emma Isleworth, that had a cheese stall with the most delicious looking cheddars, bries and blue cheeses along side chutneys and crackers. The last two stallholders that Mrs Mentary met were Scott Walter, a goatee-wearing man who sold home-brewed ales and stouts and Kelli Donovan, a jolly-looking woman with twinkly eyes who was selling artisan chocolates.

Mrs Mentary was planning what she was going to buy when Billy came running over. Someone had sabotaged the oven he used to heat the pies so he wouldn't be able to sell anything at the market today and effectively all of his stock was ruined costing him a huge amount of money. Who could have done such a nasty thing? Help Mrs Mentary find the villain!

The Suspects

1. Ginny-Flossi Brast – Innocent/Guilty, 2. Leonard Oroe – Innocent/Guilty, 3. Mona T. Ductant – Innocent/Guilty, 4. Hanna-Kelly Wotch – Innocent/Guilty, 5. Samuel Allen – Innocent/Guilty, 6. Gerald Anderson – Innocent/Guilty, 7. Liam Ham – Innocent/Guilty, 8 Dwaine R. Scour – Innocent/Guilty, 9. Quentin Jackson – Innocent/Guilty, 10. Ruth Edoven – Innocent/Guilty, 11. Lucia Borghoni – Innocent/Guilty, 12. Cat Tletro – Innocent/Guilty, 13. Ron Diseth – Innocent/Guilty, 14. Emma Isleworth – Innocent/Guilty, 15. Scott Walter – Innocent/Guilty, 16. Kelli Donovan – Innocent/Guilty.

The Mystery Tour

Your tour starts at London Fields station (overground line with trains from London Liverpool Street (www.tfl.gov.uk)).

Clue 1

Time to *dive* into the tour. Turn right onto Mentmore Terrace, turn right onto Martello Terrace and then right onto Martello Street which is *around* the park. There's something in the distance which could be quite *refreshing*.

Clue 2

Walk up Martello *Street* keeping the park on the left. That looks like another place to take *refreshment* and even get a *mixed up* cocktail or *short* drink. Perhaps its location can help remove another suspect.

Clue 3

Circle back and continue on Martello Road with the park on the left. Just in case you have *initial*ly forgotten where you are here is a reminder! Perhaps the *bottom row* can help if you follow the instructions *to the letter*.

Clue 4

It's now *time* to cross over Richmond Road and walk up Hackney Grove to Reading Lane. It's important not to *shield* yourself from any clues or you'll get *confused*.

Clue 5

*Initial*ly, turn left onto Mare Street (A107). What a *year*! This quest is such a *drama* and you are feeling like an *emperor* of destiny. Just keep following those clues *to the letter*.

Clue 6

Retrace your steps and walk south down Mare Street, the A107. You can complete this quest and things will *square* up. Don't be a doubting *Thomas*. Perhaps a cool *drink within* will help those brain cells.

Clue 7

This place is fit for a *royal princes*s. Time to *open* your mind and look *within* for more clues.

Clue 8

*Initial*ly continue walking down Mare Street. Hopefully the culprit will be *found in* less than a *year*, Time to be as strong as an *oak* and keep following the clues *to the letter*.

Clue 9

First continue walking down Mare Street, the A107 (not the A*1932*) *and* after a *second* turn right down Lamb Lane *initia*lly and then turn left onto Mentmore Terrace.

Clue 10

Head back to Mare Street and keep going south. Make sure you look past the *bulls***t and let the information *flow within*.

Clue 11

Walk down Andrews Road keeping to the *North Side*. Do you fancy *recording* some music and doing some *mixing*?

Clue 12

Continue on to Pritchard's Road. This feels like a *bridge* over troubled water. Everything has been getting *mixed up* but is smooth again now.

Clue 13

Leave the bridge and walk into Broadway Market. Time to *rebuild* your resilience. Perhaps something from the *turn of the nineteenth centur*y can help?

Clue 14

Walk up Broadway Market towards London Fields. You'll want to look *around* you at all of the amazing stalls. You are feeling very *tranquil* and *peaceful* now the tour is *flying* in the right direction.

Clue 15

You feel like this tour has given you a good *education* as you reach West*gate* Street and you are no longer a *child*. All of the *confusion* has gone.

If you walk along the right hand side of London Fields and take a right onto Martello Terrace it will take you back to Mentmore Terrace and London Fields station.

ell

Where to eat, drink, shop and play

Eating and Drinking

The Dove, 24-28 Broadway Market, E8 4QJ (www.dovepubs.com) is a traditional local pub with good hearty food with tables in the heart of the market.

The Cat & Mutton, 76 Broadway Market, E8 4RA (www.catandmutton.com) is a traditional gastropub with an ever-changing seasonal menu.

Pub on the Park, 19 Martello Street, E8 3PE (www.pubonthepark.com) is a great drinking and eating pub with brilliant views of the park, live sports and pétanque.

Chakana London, 41 Broadway Market, E8 4PH (www.chakana-restaurant.co .uk) is a cosy restaurant serving great Peruvian food and amazing cocktails.

Bella Vita, 53-57 Broadway Market, E8 4PH (www.bellavitabroadway.com) is a much-loved Italian restaurant with tasty food and tables spilling out onto the street.

Off Broadway, 63-65 Broadway Market, E8 4PH (www.offbroadway.org.uk) is a bar with cocktails, live music and street food style menu.

Aya & Suki, 62 Broadway Market, E8 4QJ (www.ayaandsuki.co.uk) is a vegan and vegetarian restaurant serving very tasty home-made dishes.

El Ganzo, 59 Broadway Market, E8 4PH (www.elgansocafe.co.uk) is a great Spanish restaurant serving tapas in a simple but chic setting.

Martello Hall, 137 Mare Street, E8 3RH (www.martellohall.com) is a bar and restaurant in an industrial setting serving wood-fired pizzas, brunches and cock-tails.

Mare Street Market, 117 Mare Street, E8 4RU (www.marestreetmarket.com) has a bar, restaurant, bottle shop and even a barbers in a warehouse style space.

Rosa's Thai, 381 Mentmore Terrace, E8 3PH (www.rosasthai.com) serves delicious Thai food in a relaxed setting.

Brat Restaurant, 374 Helmsey Place, E8 3SB (www.bratrestaurant.co.uk) serves food cooked on a woodfire in a trendy warehouse setting with a large open courtyard. See their sister coffee house Climpson & Sons Café, 67 Broadway Market, E8 4PH (www.climpsonandsons.com) in Broadway Market.

Netil360, 1 Westgate Street, E8 3RL (www.netil360.com) is a cool roof top bar with DJs, wood-fired pizzas, great drinks and saunas with amazing views.

Pavilion, 18 Broadway Market, E8 4QJ (www.pavilionbread.com) is a bread and pastry bakery with cool wood-lined interiors.

E5 Bakehouse, 396 Mentmore Terrace, E8 3PH (www.e5bakehouse.com) is an artisan bakery and café serving delicious pastries, sandwiches, breakfasts and lunches.

Pophams, 197 Richmond Road, E8 3NJ (www.pophamsbakery.com) is a fabulous bakery and coffee shop which also serves pasta in the evenings.

Shops

Aesop, 5 Broadway Market, E8 4TS (www.aesop.com) has fantastic organic skincare products and home and body fragrances.

The Broadway Bookshop, 6 Broadway Market, E8 4QJ (www.broadwaybookshophackney.com) is a great local bookshop with both new and classic titles.

Donlon Books, 75 Broadway Market, E8 4PH (www.donlonbooks.com) is a fantastic art and photography focused bookshop.

Retrouve Vintage, 23 Broadway Market, E8 4PH and 61 Wilton Way, E8 1BG (www.retrouvevintage.co.uk) has amazing vintage clothes and accessories.

Rites, 4 Broadway Market, E8 4QJ (rites.co) is the place to rent gorgeous designer dresses perfect for a wedding or party.

Fish and Flounder, 71 Broadway Market (www.finandflounder.com) is a family-run fishmonger with a wonderful selection.

Hill & Szrok, 60 Broadway Market, E8 4QJ (www.thesmallherd.co.uk) is a butcher specialising in organic, free-range meat.

Netil Market , 13-23 Westgate Street, E8 3RL (www.eatworkart.com) has a collection of food vendors and an on-site bar and coffee shop as well as regular DJs and music.

Broadway Market (www.broadwaymarket.co.uk) is open Saturdays and Sundays and provides a variety of food, fashion, homeware and art stalls.

Playing

You can walk along Regents Canal in the direction of Victoria Park and Hackney Wick one way and Haggerston and Islington in the other direction. There are a number of coffee shops and restaurants along the way and the brightly coloured barges.

London Fields Lido, London Fields West Side, E8 3EU (www.better.org.uk) has a fantastic Olympic-sized open-air swimming pool, sun-bathing area and café.

Hackney Empire, 291 Mare Street, E8 1EJ (www.hackneyempire.co.uk) is a performance arts theatre with a famous pantomime.

Hackney Picture House, 270 Mare Street, E8 1HE (www.picturehouses.com) shows both blockbuster and arthouse films and has a café, bar and restaurant.

Oslo, 14 Amhurst Road, E8 1JB (www.oslohackney.com) is a hip restaurant and bar with music and club.

MOTH Club, Valette Street, E9 6NU (www.mothclub.co.uk) is a venue hosting music and comedy performances with a club-style vibe.

Hackney Museum, 1 Reading Lane, E8 1GQ (hackney-museum.hackney.gov.uk) is a great museum on the local area with ever changing exhibitions and events.

The Viktor Wynd Museum of Curiosities, Fine Art and UnNatural History, 11 Mare Street, Cambridge Heath Road, E8 4RP (www.thelasttuesdaysociety.org) is full of weird and wonderful artwork and taxidermy and also has an absinthe bar.

Tour Ten - Wapping
Ale and Artifice

Mrs Mentary arrived at the Prospect of Whitby pub ready for the "Old Pubs of East London" tour taking place in Wapping. It was a crisp October late afternoon and the buildings looked so pretty with their brightly lit windows in the dark streets. She loved the cobbled streets with their old warehouses and wharves filled with trendy apartments and restaurants and cute coffee shops.

The tour was being lead by Joe Turner, a rugged bear of a man with messy grey hair. He was a lover of fine ale and really knew both his beers and his history. Next there were Sam Bard, a young man with a goatee, Martin Paice, man with multiple piercings, Caroline Pime, a middle aged woman with bright purple hair and Phoebe Nixon, who had a bonny face full of freckles, all from the London Microbrewing Club which loved touring historic old inns and pubs. There were four friends celebrating a fortieth birthday: Reg Imen, who was the birthday boy and wearing a massive badge to that effect, Coco T. Doback, a peroxide blonde who already looked a bit worse for wear, William Stephen, a stocky man with a swarthy complexion and Eli Can, a sun-tanned woman with dangly beer bottle-shaped earrings.

Next joining the tour were Dickens-lovers from the States who wanted to see the London of Oliver Twist; Peter Finch who had a massive camera, Walter Streather, who kept saying "how quaint" everything was and Elsie Seegh, who kept telling the men on the trip they sounded like Hugh Grant and asking if they knew Prince William.

There were four History students who were studying the importance of the Thames and London docks to the London economy (or at least this was there excuse for the pub crawl); Omar Tajid with long sleek black hair, Liam Blig who was exceptionally tall and skinny, Pierre Montague, who had a huge belly laugh and Boyce Ickstie, who looked a bit bored and kept looking at their phone. Finally, there was Tim Brompson from the Tourist Information Board who was going to potentially promote the tour if he thought it was any good.

The tour was highly engaging and Mrs Mentary along with the rest of the group very much enjoyed the half pint of beer provided at every drinking establishment on route. Peter was snapping away like a member of the paparazzi with his massive-lensed camera which annoyed quite a lot of the group since he kept barging in front of people. The group was all quite merry by the time they finally returned to the Prospect of Whitby and all stayed for more chat and merriment.

The group were gradually dispersing when Peter suddenly swore at the top of his voice. His very expensive camera was missing! Who had stolen it? Solve the clues and help Mrs Mentary find the culprit!

The Suspects

1. Joe Turner – Innocent/Guilty, 2. Sam Bard – Innocent/Guilty, 3. Martin Paice – Innocent/Guilty, 4. Caroline Pime – Innocent/Guilty, 5. Phoebe Nixon – Innocent/Guilty, 6. Reg Imen – Innocent/Guilty, 7. Coco T. Doback – Innocent/Guilty, 8. William Stephen – Innocent/Guilty, 9. Eli Can – Innocent/Guilty, 10. Walter Streather - Innocent/Guilty, 11. Elsie Seegh – Innocent/Guilty, 12. Omar Tajid – Innocent/Guilty, 13. Liam Blig – Innocent/Guilty, 14. Pierre Montague – Innocent/Guilty, 15. Boyce Ickstie – Innocent/Guilty, 16. Tim Brompson – Innocent/Guilty

The Mystery Tour

Your trail starts at Wapping Station, Meeting House Alley Poplar, E1W 3PA which is on London Overground (www.tfl.gov.uk).

Clue 1

First, look *within* the station next to the *river.* Don't get *tunnel* vision or think the quest is *design*ed to be *beneath* you or you'll be *driven* mad.

Clue 2

*Initial*ly, turn right onto Wapping High Street and then right onto Wapping Wall. The *prospect* of *start*ing this tour is daunting. You'll need to keep your *wits by* you and follow the clues *to the letter* to complete this *year*.

Clue 3

Sometimes you can be a bit of a *bird* brain! Is that a *crossing* or a *flight* of *steps within*?

Clue 4

Keep walking up Wapping Wall and cross over Shadwell Basin keeping *within* the pedestrian part of the bridge. You need to be well *drill*ed to solve this *great* tour which feels like being in the *wars*.

Clue 5

Take a right onto the Thames Path and walk to the river. Breathe in the *fresh air*. Have you got a *window* to the solution yet?

Clue 6

Once you've *explore*d and seen some of the boats *sail*ing down the river *navigate* away from the river and *cross* over to the park. Perhaps *two brothers* can help remove the next suspect?

Clue 7

Exit the park and walk down The Highway (A1203) heading towards central London. Is it time for some *divine* intervention? No, you need to be an *architect* of your own destiny and *build* on your previous success.

Clue 8

Walk along the *dock* and then take a right at the narrow channel of water to go into Wapping Woods. Exit the woods continuing along the channel of water to get to Wapping Lane. Is there a clue here? There is no *smoke* without fire as they say!

Clue 9

Walk down the canal past the two large boats and cross the second foot bridge on the left to get to Waterman Way. Turn right to *transport* yourself to *within* Reardon Street. Will this street be *fruit*ful so you can give thanks for your daily *bread*?

Clue 10

Continue down Reardon Street. You're pleased with your *glory*ous *advancement* and feel like holding a *festival*!

Clue 11

Continue to Watts Street. This *old star painter* will help you in your *secret* quest. Perhaps taking a drink in a *booth* at the local pub might help?

Clue 12

Cross over Wapping Gardens exiting on Tench Street and then continue on until it becomes Scandrett Street. This tour feels like being back at *school*! Did you behave like a *saint* and *ignore the girls?* Were you good at your *numbers*?

Clue 13

Turn left onto Wapping High Street. It *sounds a bit like* the *far east* around here. Take the *steps* you can to find the *opening* in the search.

Clue 14

Continue along Wapping High Street. This tour feels like it has been going on for *over 200* years! Perhaps the people who have *protect*ed our waterways can help you from getting *mixed up*?

Clue 15

Continue along Wapping High Street. It's time to *fly* ahead and *rise from the ashes*! Just *contain* your joy when you eliminate the final suspect and solve the crime! You are a short distance from Wapping Station where you started your tour.

—ell—

Where to eat, drink, shop and play

There is a good selection of fine old pubs, restaurants and cafés in Wapping. There are not many shops or boutiques with the major shopping centre of Canary Wharf so close by.

Eating and Drinking

The Prospect of Whitby, 57 Wapping Wall, E1 3SH (www.greeneking.co.uk) is a historic pub with amazing river views, traditional pub food and cask ales.

Town of Ramsgate, 62 Wapping High Street, E1W 2PN (www.townoframsgat e.pub) is a sixteenth century riverside pub with food, real ales, wines and cocktails seeped in history.

Bistro Bardot, 1 Green Bank, E1W 2PA (www.bistrobardot.co.uk) is an atmospheric, candle-lit bistro set in an historic pub, The Turk's Head.

Wapping Tavern, 70-80 Wapping Lane, E1W 2RT (www.wappingtavern.co.uk) is a friendly pub and restaurant housed in an old spice factory with pub games like table tennis and pool serving gastro pub food.

Il Bordello, Metropolitan Wharf, 70 Wapping Wall, E1W 3SS (www.ilbordell o.com) is an excellent Italian restaurant serving traditional dishes in a bustling white-washed dining room with a chic copper bar.

Il Bacino, 21 Wapping Lane, E1W 2RN (www.ilbianco.co.uk) is another fabulous Italian with clean-lined modern interiors and excellent food.

Urban Baristas, 138 Wapping High Street, E1W 3PA (www.urbanbaristas.co.uk) create their own coffee blends and also serve great coffee, and sweet and savoury baked goods in a café and a kiosk next to the train station.

Cinnamon Coffee Shop, 103 Wapping Lane E1W 2RW (Facebook page) serves coffee, shakes and snacks in a cosy setting.

Playing

The Thames Path runs next to the river and you can walk to St Katharine's Docks and the Tower of London one direction and Limehouse and Canary Wharf the other direction.

There are a number of old "stairs" that take you down to the beaches by the Thames such as Wapping New Stairs, Wapping Dock Stairs and New Crane Stairs. King Henry's Stairs takes you to Execution Dock where pirates and smugglers were hung.

The walk from Shadwell Basin along the canal is interesting with two boat replicas on display next to Tobacco Docks, an events space. There is a Saturday market with music and food stalls next to Shadwell Basin.

Shadwell Basin Outdoor Activity Centre, 3-4 Shadwell Pierhead, Glamis Road, E1W 3TD (www.shadwell-basin.co.uk) offers dingy sailing course on the Thames and canoeing courses on Shadwell Basin.

Tower of London, EC3N 4AB (www.hrp.org.uk) is the fine medieval castle which houses the crown jewels and is protected by the famous Beefeaters.

Thames River Police Museum, Wapping Police Station, Wapping High Street, E1W 2NE (www.thamespolicemuseum.org.uk) is a quirky museum housed in a room in the police station which you can arrange to visit by appointment.

Jack the Ripper Museum, 12 Cable Street, Aldgate, E1 8JG (www.jacktherippe rmuseum.com) is a museum with artefacts and information about the notorious Victorian killer.

Wilton's Music Hall, 1 Graces Alley, E18JB (www.wiltons.org.uk) is a beautiful old music hall with great theatre, comedy and music productions and bar and restaurant. It is very atmospheric.

Troxy, 490 Commercial Road, E1 0HX (www.troxy.co.uk) is a live music venue in an old art deco theatre.

Escape Room London, 412 Commercial Road, E1 0LB (www.escape-london.c o.uk) provides multiple escape rooms for those that enjoy puzzles.

Tour Eleven - Belsize Park

A Dramatic Deceipt

Mrs Mentary was in beautiful Belsize Park to attend the preview night of a new play about twenty-something Londoners set in the 1980s by brilliant young playwrite, Chris T. Agaffa. Mrs Mentary had a few hours to kill when she arrived at Swiss Cottage station on the chilly Wednesday afternoon in November and had a wander around the white stucco and red brick-lined streets of the leafy neighbourhood.

When she arrived at the theatre the preview was about to start but there was a huge argument taking place between Chris and the director, Able Noil. Chris, who had been in the States for the past few months, was not happy with Able's interpretation of Donny, the main character. They thought that Hamish Rupert Henderson. who was playing Donny was not charismatic enough and didn't have the steely determination that Donny had at the height of the booming Thatcherite eighties.

Cleo Morture, Hamish's girlfriend in both the play and real life, was furious with Chris and was giving them a mouthful of expletives. Kaye Nein, a stunning brunette who was playing a femme fatale in the play piped up and said that she agreed with Chris and did not think the audience would believe that Donny could seduce her.

At this point in time a number of the supporting cast were looking decidedly annoyed; Bert Pol, a tall dark-haired man playing Donny's best friend, Tim Benson, a stocky bald man playing Donny's boss, Daphne Pine, an elderly woman with dyed red hair playing Donny's mother and Aly Pen, a petite woman with peroxide blonde curls, playing Donny's Secretary.

"Chris and Able, the press are here, " said Kate Ushose, a sensible-looking young woman who was the assistant director.

"And they'll roast us in the reviews!" yelled Chris.

The stage manager, an eagle-nosed man called Alf Reehos, at this point interrupted and suggested to Chris that the discussion continue in another room at which point Chris exploded.

"The support actors are just not gold enough for this production!" they yelled at two men, Ross Lyn and Walt Lohn dressed in pin-striped power suits and two women, Wendy Casper Adams and Sunita Mani with poodle perms, bright red lipstick and massive shoulder pads. "They're supposed to be power driven yuppies but have as much energy as a dead hedgehog!".

An authoritative man dressed entirely in black came into the room. Mrs Mentary understood it was Barry Li, the highly regarded producer of the show. "Enough, Chris," he said quietly and things calmed down.

Mrs Mentary attended the first night performance and all went well and the critics loved the over the top production. But where was Chris? In bed with a very nasty bout of food poisoning brought on by a gift of chocolates they had received. It was obvious there had been some foul play afoot but who was responsible? It is up to you to help Mrs Mentary find out!

The Suspects

1. Chris T. Agaffa – Innocent/Guilty, 2. Able Noil – Innocent/Guilty. 3. Hamish Rupert Henderson – Innocent/Guilty, 4. Cleo Morture – Innocent/Guilty, 5. Kaye Nein – Innocent/Guilty, 6. Bert Pol – Innocent/Guilty, 7. Tim Benson – Innocent/Guilty, 8. Daphne Pine – Innocent/Guilty, 9. Aly Pen – Innocent/Guilty, 10. Kate Ushose – Innocent/Guilty, 11. Alf Reehos – Innocent/Guilty, 12. Ross Lyn – Innocent/Guilty, 13. Walt Lohn – Innocent/Guilty, 14. Wendy Casper Adams – Innocent/Guilty, 15. Sunita Mani – Innocent/Guilty, 16. Barry Li – Innocent/Guilty.

The Mystery Tour

Your trail starts at Swiss Cottage station which is on the Jubilee Line on the London Underground (www.tfl.gov.uk).

Clue 1

Take the exit which takes you out on the east side where Hampstead Theatre is (towards *Camden Town*). Walk up Adamson Road. Some of these doors are *paint*ed a nice shade of b*lue*? I wonder what the houses are like *within*.

Clue 2

Turn left onto *Cross*field Road then left onto Lancaster Grove and right onto Belsize Park. You are looking for some *divine teaching*. Perhaps there is a *room* dedicated to this that can help remove the *confusion*?

Clue 3

Continue walking up Belsize Park and then turn left into Belsize Terrace and the lovely Belsize Village area. You may want to take some time to visit some of the shops, cafés and restaurants here before continuing your tour. Then walk up Belsize Lane that turns in Ornan Road until you are close to Haverstock Hill. There seem a lot of *mansion*s. Is there *royalty* about? Keep going with the quest and b*lock* out all distractions!

Clue 4

Turn left onto Haverstock Hill and then turn right down a path on the right which has the churchyard on the left. You're so tired you may need some *medical assistance within* this place?

Clue 5

Turn right onto Pond Street. You'll deserve a *crown* with *white* diamonds and *red* rubies *within* if you solve this mystery as the clues a*rose*.

Clue 6

Initially, you thought you'd need to be *nurse*d along with this myste*ry* to solve it in a *day*. But a *royal* has helped you *open* yourself up to success.

Clue 7

Walk down to South End Green. This is a *monument*al quest! Perhaps another person *associated with mysteries* can provide *inspiration*?

Clue 8

Walk up South End Road and taking the next road on the left after Heath Hurst Road. Perhaps another *writer* can help you put things *in order* so you can get a full *house* with the clues!

Clue 9

Turn left onto Downshire Hill walking up to Rosslyn Hill. *Sounds like* there might be some *piggies* and *frogs* around here?

Clue 10

Turn left onto Rosslyn Hill and walk down it. You'll initially want to *follow the rules to the letter* so you don't end up here during the *year*.

Clue 11

Walk down Rosslyn Hill as it turns back into Haverstock Hill. What's that imposing place on the right and can it help your brain feel less *scrambled* and stop you going around in *circles*?

Clue 12

Continue down Haverstock Hill to Antrim Grove and have a little *play within*. You are not feeling too *well* (not un*common* on these mystery tours when everything feels a *bit backwards*).

Clue 13

Return back to Antrim Grove. You're *reading* the clues and finding out a lot of *information* which is resolving the *confusion*.

Clue 14

Walk down Antrim Grove and turn right onto England's Lane. Walk down England's Lane then cross over to Eton Avenue. Despite *initially* seeing *red* you've been a *brick*. Not much *left* to go now.

Clue 15

Continue walking down Eton Avenue. You'll feeling *thirsty* and you've been at *sixes* and sevens! What are those rather *menacing creatures* you can see? Perhaps they will help you remove the final suspect and solve the crime!

If you continue down Eton Avenue you will return to Swiss Cottage station.

—*ell*—

Where to eat, drink, shop and play

There are four great areas to eat, drink and shop on the tour, Belsize Village, South End Green, Haverstock Hill and England's Lane.

Eating and Drinking

Jamon Jamon, 177 Haverstock Hill, Belsize Park, NW3 4QS (www.jamonjamo n.uk.com) serves fantastic tapas and Spanish dishes.

Mitsuryu, 9 South End Rd, NW3 2PT (www.mitsuryu.co.uk) is a relaxed Japanese restaurant with outdoor tables offering sushi, meat dishes, gyoza and rice bowls.

Cinder, 66 Belsize Ln, Belsize Park, NW3 5BJ (www.cinderrestaurant.co.uk) specialises in beautiful meat and vegetable dishes cooked over an open fire. It's all delicious!

Caldesi, 29 Belsize Ln, Belsize Park, NW3 5AS (www.caldesi.com) serves stunning Italian food and amazing cocktails.

The Roebuck, 15 Pond St, NW3 2PN (www.roebuckhampstead.com) is a nineteenth century pub with cosy fireplace and leather armchairs and a stylish heated beer garden. It serves gastropub style comfort food like truffle fries and apple and blackberry crumble.

The Washington, 50 England's Lane,   NW3 4UE (www.thewashingtonhamp-stead.co.uk) is a wood-panelled Victorian pub with embossed red ceiling, serving seasonal British food and a great selection of beers and wines.

The Magdala Tavern, 2a South Hill Park, NW3 2SB (www.themagdala.co.uk) is a lovely local pub with great food and excellent beer garden.

Mileto Caffé, Pears Building, Rosslyn Hill, NW3 2PP (www.miletocaffe.com) is an Italian family-run café serving delicious coffees, pastries and lunches which is a firm favourite amongst locals.

Oliver's Village Café, 92 Belsize Lane, NW3 5BE (www.oliversvillagecafe.com) serves great breakfasts, brunches, lunches and cakes in a warm friendly setting.

Euphorium Bakery. 45 South End Road, NW3 2QB and Hillfield Mansions, 211 Haverstock Hill, Belsize Park, NW3 4QN (www.euphorium.uk.com) has great coffees, smoothies, baked goods, breakfasts and lunches in a Scandinavian-style interior.

England's Lane Café, 2 England's Lane, Belsize Park, NW3 4TG (www.engla ndslanecafe.com) serves amazing breakfasts, brunches, sandwiches and salads all with an Antipodean twist.

Shops

Daunt Books, Hillfield Mansions, 193 Haverstock Hill, Belsize Park, NW3 4QL (www.dauntbooks.co.uk) is a fantastic book shop which stocks all of the latest releases and classics as well as holding regular events.

Bourne's Fishmongers, 31 Belsize Lane, Belsize Park, NW3 5AS (www.bournesf ish.co.uk) stocks the finest sustainable fish and seafood.

Pomona, 179 Haverstock Hill, Belsize Park, NW3 4QS (www.pomonafoods.co .uk) is a delicatessen serving delicious products such as cheeses, charcuterie and wines.

Artichoke, 20 England's Lane, Belsize Park, NW3 4TL (Facebook page) is an amazing green grocers that also sells flowers and has a juice bar.

Barrett Butchers, 40 England's Lane, Belsize Park, NW3 4UE (www.barrettsbu tchers.co.uk) is a family run butchers with an amazing selection of meat, game, pies and cheese.

Playing

Hampstead Heath (www.hampsteadheath.net) is a huge area of parkland which has swimming ponds and great views of London. Whilst there visit Kenwood House, Hampstead Lane, NW3 7JR (www.english-heritage.org.uk) which is a beautiful house with an amazing art collection.

Visit 2 Willow Road, NW3 1TH (www.nationaltrust.org.uk) Erno Goldfinger's innovative 1939 Modernist house includes his modern art and furniture collections.

Hampstead Hill Lido (www.cityoflondon.gov.uk) Parliament Hill Fields, Gordon House Rd, London NW5 1LT is a lovely outside lido.

Keats House, 40 England's Lane, Belsize Park, NW3 4UE (www.cityoflondon.gov.uk) is the beautiful Regency villa where Romantic poet John Keats found inspiration, friendship and love which is open to the public.

Hampstead Theatre, Eton Avenue, Swiss Cottage, NW3 3EU is a fantastic (www.hampsteadtheatre.com) is a leading producing theatre that has two stages and aims to offer West End production values at a fraction of the cost.

Everyman Cinema, 203 Haverstock Hill, Belsize Park, NW3 4QG (www.everymancinema.com) is a lovely theatre-style cinema with waiter service showing both new releases and classic films with a regular diary of events.

Tour Twelve - Hampstead
The Holly-loving Highwayman

M rs Mentary arrived at Hampstead as small flakes of snow were starting to fall. It was five-thirty at the start of December and she was here to cover a wreath-making tour in Hampstead Heath. The first part of the tour would involve collecting berries, fir cones and other foliage from the heath with the second part involving the actual making of the wreath in one of Hampstead's beautiful old inns.

As Mrs Mentary entered the inn she was greeted by Lydia Armitage, a well-known local florist who was leading the tour. She was joined by her partner, Jonathon Scelb, a local historian who would be also be giving the participants some history about the area including the infamous highwaymen who targeted carriages on their way to London. The first participants to arrive were Wendy Howell-Lough, Lena Domin and Ria T. Sal, three well-spoken yummy mummies who were having a girls night out and all looked incredibly glamorous in cashmere and pearls. Mrs Mentary imagined their wreaths would be taking pride of place on brightly coloured doorways of grand Georgian or Victorian houses.

Next to arrive were a group of friends from the University of the Third Age; Al Swort, Lawrence Deaiche and Rob Ertlo, all wearing novelty Christmas jumpers. Rob laughed that he was hopeless at anything crafty and he imagined his wife would be putting his wreath straight into the green waste bin. Mica Lobser, Matt Hamish Tosit and Den Bathsan all worked in a local estate agents and were on a work do. They had already started drinking at lunchtime and were somewhat merry when they arrived. Mrs Mentary thought it was likely that their wreaths would end up in the bin too if they didn't impale themselves on the holly first given their lack of general coordination.

Ben Tonlowce and Katherine Ferrel were two students who appeared to be on a date. Mrs Mentary thought it was pretty brave to try any type of craft activity on a romantic occasion given the opportunity for outbursts of frustration. Finally there were Shirley Daner. Ollga Teho and Sue Laurier who were from the local arts society and were keen to express their creativity in the process with one participant even asking if it was possible to make a deconstructed wreath which received a withering look from Lydia.

The participants put on their gardening gloves and set off into the heath with torches and secateurs. They started collecting their leaves, holly and cones in baskets whilst Jonathon handed out mulled wine from a flask and told them some tales of intrigues about the thieves and vagabonds that used to frequent the woods. Once sufficient materials had been collected they returned to the pub where they were shown how to bind the foliage to moss-covered wire-frames by Lydia and wire the berries and cones. Lydia also helped them tie elegant bows for the bottom of their wreaths. Some wreaths certainly looked better than others at the end but everyone was pretty satisfied with what they were taking home including Mrs Mentary who loved the reds and golds in her wreath.

Mrs Mentary carried her wreath carefully to her car and was fumbling for her keys in her handbag when she heard a noise behind her. There was someone with a black hat and scarf around their face. "Give me your bag!" they said brandishing what looked like a knife. Mrs Mentary found her alarm in her bag and a shrill noise immediately went off. The would-be thief immediately ran off and Mrs Mentary was left feeling very shaken.

Who was this modern-day highwayperson? It's up to you to help Mrs Mentary find the clues and work it out.

—ell—

The Suspects

1. Lydia Armitage – Innocent/Guilty, 2. Jonathon Scelb – Innocent/Guilty, 3. Wendy Howell-Lough – Innocent/Guilty, 4. Lena Domin – Innocent/Guilty, 5. Ria T. Sal – Innocent/Guilty, 6. Al Swort – Innocent/Guilty, 7. Lawrence Deaiche – Innocent/Guilty, 8. Rob Ertlo – Innocent/Guilty, 9. Mica Lobser – Innocent/Guilty, 10. Matt Hamish Tosit – Innocent/Guilty, 11. Den Bathsan – Innocent/Guilty, 12. Ben Tonlowce – Innocent/Guilty, 13. Katherine Ferrel – Innocent/Guilty, 14. Shirley Daner – Innocent Guilty, 15. Ollga Teho – Innocent/Guilty, 16. Sue Laurier – Innocent/Guilty.

—ell—

The Mystery Tour

Your mystery tour starts at Hampstead underground station which is on the Norther Line (www.tfl.gov.uk).

Clue 1

Turn left onto Heath Street and take a right into *Church* Row. You're feeling a little *grave* about finding this con-*artist*. Is that a *policeman* that can help get things *in order*?

Clue 2

Turn right onto Frognal Gardens. It's important to *act* quickly *or* the culprit will get away. Just dig deep *within* and don't get things *backwards*.

Clue 3

Continue up Frognal Gardens and turn right onto Frognal. You're doing well *contra*ry to *alt*ernative *o*pinions and feel like *sing*ing is *in order*!

Clue 4

Turn right down Mount Vernon. Is it time to find some *treasure within* so you don't feel alone like an *island*? Thank goodness Mrs Mentary had not been *kidnapped* instead!

Clue 5

Turn right down so you are *within* Holly Walk. Time to *pray* for more clue*s to* find Mrs *M*ent*ary's* thief! Is the *writing on the wall*?

Clue 6

Retrace your steps and turn right onto Mount Vernon. You are feeling a bit *blue* now. Is it a *sign* of the cold or your *physiology*? A chem*ist* would know and stop the *mix up*.

Clue 7

Continue down Mount Vernon and then turn left onto Frognal Rise and right onto Windmill Hill. *Sounds like* this tour could be of *national* importance. Don't *trust* anyone!

Clue 8

At *last* turn left onto Hampstead Grove and walk up to the street *name*d Admiral's Walk. By *George*, is this a *sign*? *Sounds like* it could help remove the next suspect.

Clue 9

Turn left onto Admiral's Walk. To solve this mystery tour you've got to have *novel* thinking *within* and *play* your cards *right*.

Clue 10

Turn right onto Windmill Hill (*spotting* John Constable's summer residence *within* on the way) then right onto Lower Terr*ace* and continue when it becomes Hampstead Grove. Is it time to look to the *stars* for the solution to this mystery tour?

Clue 11

Take a left path to get to the pond and West Heath Road. At this point walk into the heath and Golders Hill Park on your left heading for the Hill Garden and Pergola and enjoy the views and take a break from mystery solving.

Once you have finished *1st* head for Iverforth Close and then turn right onto North End Way. It's time to get back to the *initial* soap opera and *lever*age the clues to find the culprit!

Clue 12

There is a path across the road. Follow it until it North End Avenue and then Wildwood Terrace taking the path *in order* to get to Wildwood Road which becomes Hampstead Way where you turn left passing Wyldes Close on your left. There are some stunning houses around here with some amazing *architec*ture.

Clue 13

Retrace your steps and walk *within* Wildwood Road with the *estates* of the heath on either side. Take a path on the left as the road bends around to get to Spaniards Road *passing through* more woodland. Turn left onto *Spaniards* Road and walk up to the *entrance* and *gate* of the inn. You feel you are paying a *price* to find the culprit.

Clue 14

You have two options now. You can either walk back down Spaniards Road towards Hampstead village to a take a path on the left just before the war memorial or you can walk in the opposite direction along Spaniards Road to take the Kenwood House entrance into the heath and walk along the paths in the heath. In both cases your destination is the end of the Vale of Health road furthest away from Hampstead village. The latter is a nice walk but takes around 15 minutes longer but you may want to stop at Kenwood House for a visit or grab a snack in the restaurant.

As you walk down the Vale of Health you think the tour is coming together like pure *poet*ry. The clues may be *novel* but they are helping to solve the he*ist*.

Clue 15

Walk to the end of the Vale of Health and turn left onto East Heath Road and then right into *Well* Walk and then right so you are within Flask Walk. This is a lovely part of Hampstead so *wash* away your worries *soak* up the gorgeous buildings in the ten-minute walk. You need to eliminate the last suspect. Perhaps *three fat ladies* can help?.

If you continue down Flask Walk and turn right onto the main high street you will be back at Hampstead underground station.

Where to eat, drink, shop and play

There are some lovely eating, drinking and shopping opportunities in Hampstead with some well-known upmarket high street brands as well as independent boutiques. Definitely a great place for some serious Christmas shopping!

Eating and Drinking

The Holly Bush, 22 Holly Mount, NW3 6SG (www.hollybushhampstead.co.uk) is a traditional eighteenth century pub nestled down a side street with cost wood-panelled interiors, log fires, courtyard garden and tasty gastropub food.

The Duke of Hamilton, 23-25 New End, NW3 1JD (www.locipubs.com) is an eighteenth century pub with opulent traditional interiors in bold colours which has a jazz club in the basement.

The Wells Tavern, 30 Well Walk, NW3 1BX (www.thewellshampstead.co.uk) is a stunning gastropub in a Georgian house with delicious food and upstairs and downstairs dining areas.

The Old Bull and Bush, North End Way, NW3 7HE (www.thebullandbush.co.uk) is a great gastropub with modern, airy interiors, delicious food and an outside courtyard for al fresco eating and drinking.

The Spaniards Inn, Spaniards Road, NW3 7JJ (www.thespaniardshampstead.co.uk) is a historical pub in the heart of the heath with beautiful traditional interiors, outside terrace and great food.

28 Church Row, 28 Church Row, NW3 6UP (www.28churchrow.com) is an intimate restaurant serving Italian and Spanish-inspired small plates.

Villa Bianca, 1 Perrin's Court, NW3 1QS (www.villabiancagroup.com) is a romantic Italian restaurant serving classic dishes with al fresco dining in the summer.

Ginger & White, 4a, 5a Perrin's Court, London NW3 1QU (www.gingerandwhite.com) is a trendy café serving artisan coffee, gorgeous cakes, toasties and lovely shakes and smoothies.

Mani's, 12 Perrin's Court, NW3 1QS (Facebook page) is a laid back café with great breakfasts, brunches and lunches with some outside tables.

New York Café , 84 Heath Street, NW3 1DN (www.newyorkcafe.co.uk) has a great vibe and serves really good breakfasts, brunches and lunches,

La Creperie de Hampstead, 77a Hampstead High Street, NW3 1RE (www.lacreperiedehampstead.com) is a Hampstead institution serving tasty sweet and savoury crepes from a small kiosk in the high street.

Venchi Chocolate and Gelato, 65 Hampstead High Street, NW3 1QP (uk.venchi.com) serves gorgeous chocolates and gelato.

Shopping

Hampstead has a lot of very good high end or designer shops such as Space NK, Reiss, Whistles, Maje, Zadig & Voltaire, American Vintage, Sandro, Toast, Sweaty Betty, Tara Jarmon and Free People. It also has some boutique and independent shopping.

Trilogy Stores, 52-54 Heath Street, NW3 1DL (www.trilogystores.co.uk) is a ladies fashion shop stocking brands such as Vanessa Bruno and RIXO.

Linea Fashion, (www.lineafashion.com) stocks a good selectin of men and women's designer fashion from labels such as Missoni, Moncler and Velvet.

Aesop, 41 Hampstead High Street, NW3 1QE (www.aesop.com) has fantastic organic skincare products and home and body fragrances.

Dinny Hall, 18 Hampstead High Street, NW3 1PX (www.dinnyhall.com) sells stunning jewellery using precious and semi-precious stones.

Lords in Hampstead, 22 Heath Street, NW3 6TE (www.lordsathome.com) is a stylist homewares shop.

The Hampstead Butcher & Providore, 56 Rosslyn Hill, NW3 1ND (www.hampsteadbutcher.com) sells great cuts of meat, wines and deli goods.

Borough Kitchen Cook Shop, 1B, 1C Hampstead High Street, NW3 1RG (www.boroughkitchen.com) sells a fantastic range of cookware and bakeware.

Playing

The heath is a wonderful place to take a stroll. Parliament Hill has fine views of central London and you can enjoy the bathing ponds (www.cityoflondon.gov.uk) .

Kenwood House, Hampstead Lane, NW3 7JR (www.english-heritage.org.uk) is a fine seventeenth century house and grounds with restored interiors and important artworks. Great café and restaurant with indoor and outdoor seating.

Fenton House and Garden, Hampstead Grove, NW3 6RT (www.nationaltrust.org.uk) is a beautiful former merchant's house with lovely gardens and a fine collection of musical instruments.

Burgh House, New End Square, NW3 1LT (www.burghhouse.org.uk) is a stunning Queen Anne mansion and has a museum, gallery and events space and also a great café.

The Duke of Hamilton, 23-25 New End, NW3 1JD (www.locipubs.com) has a
great jazz club in the basement.

Everyman Cinema, 5 Holly Bush Vale, NW3 6TX (www.everymancinema.com)
is an intimate cinema with two screens, plush seating and a bar. It shows blockbuster and arthouse films and has a great programme of events.

Solutions

P lease find the solutions to each clue below and the name of the culprit which is within the answers to each tour so you don't accidentally see the culprit's name too early.

Victoria Park and Bethnal Green

Clue 1: There is a memorial to two people who tried to save others in a house "fire" which mentions C.E. "Fox". The suspect's name is within the text - Nat Temp. Clue 2: You are "finding your inner child" at the Museum of Childhood which is part of the Victoria and Albert group of museums (see the large V&A on the building). This gives you the next suspect's name - Victory Andalbert. Clue 3: York Hall which is a leisure centre ("time to exercise" and "fit") is opposite which is an anagram ("confused") of the suspect to remove - Karly Hol. Clue 4: On the right is the "Assumption" "Prior"y which has a "year" above the door 1912 which if you translate "to the letter" is S and L which are the "initials" of the next suspect to remove - Sally Letterman. Clue 5: There are two dog statues entitled "The Dogs of Alcibiades" presented by "Lady" Regnart which gives the name of the next suspect to remove - Reg Nart. Clue 6: There is a drinking fountain and cattle trough. The suspect's name is "around" the word trough - Robert Rought. Clue 7: There is a stone with a "star" on it in memory of Capt Lionel Lee a Second World War Jewish "hero" from Hackney. The suspect's name is "within" the inscription on the stone - Rose N. Deat. Clue 8: There are plaques with the letters V.P. standing for "Victor""ia" "Park" . These are the initials of the suspect - Vinay Parjeet. Clue 9: Bow (take a "bow", use a bow and arrow to "take a shot") Wharf is on the left. The suspect's name is an anagram - Rob W. Whaf. Clue 10: You have reached "Old" "Ford" "Lock" and the suspect's name is an anagram ("mixed up") - Rolf Doldock. Culprit: Antony V. Dell – He was very jealous of the elaborate flush mechanism feeling he had never achieved such sophistication in his puppet creations. Clue 11: The "initials" "V.R."("royal") are on the "bridge" which are also the "initials" of the next suspect to remove - Venetia Rouse. Clue 12: There is a flag stone Jubilee "Green""way" in the "ground" which identifies the next suspect to remove - Lee Juby. Clue 13: There is an entrance ("enter") to the park which also refers to "Tower" Hamlets ("hero fit for Shakespeare"). The suspect's name is an anagram ("mixed up") of this – Matthew Orles. Clue 14: There is a sign for an old pub in the red cricket building on the corner of Bishops Way - Arabian ("Middle" "East") "Arms". "Within" this is the next suspect - Rabi Anar. Clue 15: On the old town hall there is a "stone" laid by "May""or" A.F. Barnard which also mentions "build"ing "committee". The "year" mentioned is 1909 which is S and I "to the letter" which are the "initials" of the last suspect to remove - Sarah Ingrids.

Blackheath

Clue 1: There is a house on the right of Tranquil Vale with the engraved words "established" 1800 and "rebuilt" 1885. If you translate the numbers 1885 "to the letter" you get "R H E" which are the "initials" of the next suspect to be removed - Rupert Hammond-Edgar. Clue 2: There is a water fountain ("refreshment") which has an inscription when it was erected in "1897" which contains the words "gracious majesty" that have inspired the name of the next suspect - Grace Usma Jesty. Clue 3: The location to "pray" is "All Saints" Church which is an anagram ("confused") of the suspect - Niall Tass. Clue 4: Stay in the churchyard ("Continue to seek godly inspiration") and you will see a "four-leaved clover" shaped inscription on the side of the church which mentions the "fifth" Earl of Dartmouth – Earl Dartmouth. Clue 5: There is a building with a "blue" plaque which commemorates the founding quarters of the Mass Observation, a "pioneering" "social survey". The suspects name is an anagram of "social survey" - Russel Ociavy. Clue 6: There is a "red" "letter" "box" with "GR" on it which inspires and uses the initials of the next suspect - Georgiana Royale. Clue 7: There is a blue plaque to polar ("cold", "North Pole") explorer Sir James Clark Ross on one of the houses - Ross Clark James. Clue 8: There is a house with the date 1806 on it which when you translate the numbers "to the letter" is R and F which are the ""initials" of the next innocent person - Rosalind French. Clue 9: On Ranger's House there is an inscription to Philip the "fourth" Earl of Chesterfield a "state"s"man" and author ("right" sounds like "write) - Philip Chesterfield. Clue 10: There is a plaque in the wall marking 0 degrees "long""itude" or the Prime Meridian. The suspects name is an anagram ("confused") of Prime Meridian - Meridie Priman. Clue 11: By the entrance to Greenwich Park is a plaque to the Cornish "rebels" that "march"ed to London in the fifteenth century. The plaque is donated by Delabole Slate and the suspects name is within that - Del Aboles. Culprit: Terry Voles. He had been spurned by Marielle in favour of Earl and wanted to ruin her career. Clue 12: The Millennium Circle is a paved area in the shape of a "circle" in the middle of the common. It has the names of the respective "fields" of the common on it. If you "ignore" Old "Donkey" Pit the suspect's name is constructed from the remaining fields - Lincoln Kentchurch. Clue 13: There is a water fountain ("thirsty" and "fountain") next to Prince of Wales Pond which references the month "March". It has M R A on it which are the "initials" of the next suspect to remove - Mary Rebecca Armitage. Clue 14: There is a house with a "shield" on it which has a

Knight ("night")'s helmet and fish on it. The motto is "Nihil Sine Labore" which has the suspect's name "within" - Nel Abor. Clue 15: The Clarendon Hotel is on the left ("place to rest your weary head"). It is an anagram ("scrambled") of the last suspect to remove - Clare N. Hoonteld.

Wandsworth

Clue 1: There is an engraved stone on a house which says Marlborough "Terrace" 1881 ("palindrome date") H.J.C. The latter are the "initials" of the suspect to remove – Holly-Jane Carlton. Clue 2: All of the houses have "leaves" decoration in this street. Leaves is "within" the next suspect's name – Lea Vesper. Clue 3: There are three named houses ("named trio") on the "bend", Rose Cottage, Lansdown House and Gordon House, which together make the name of the next innocent person – Rose Landsdown-Gordon. Clue 4: There is a building with a clock ("time") on it with the date 1888 ("three fat ladies"). It has a "blue" plaque on it to Sir Hugh Walpole marking the home of the "Book""er" "Prize" winner. The next suspect's name is within the wording on the plaque – Gina Lhom. Clue 5: You are walking down Melody ("tuneful") Road. The next innocent person's name is made up of two of the side street names – Jessica Quarry. Clue 6: The Windmill ("wind", "sail") is next to John Archer Way. The next suspect's name is an anagram ("confusion") – Willem Thind. Clue 7: There are plaques on the Royal Victoria Building mentioning the "builder" V. Alonso and "owner" P. Tutton which together make up the name of the next suspect to remove – Alonso Tutton. Culprit: Bryony Smart. She had clashed with Hilda a number of times over a Christmas tree that used too much tinsel and a scarecrow that was wearing gold hot pants and wanted to teach Hilda a lesson. Clue 8: There is a bowling green ("game") next to the café which is an anagram ("mix up") of the name of the next innocent person – Ginger Bowlen. Clue 9: Harbury Villa ("named residence", "could be in sunny Spain") is on the right and the suspect's name is "around" this – Shar Buryman. Clue 10: Northcote Church ("heaven") made of "brick" is on the left. Within the wall is a "foundation" "stone" laid by Robert Hayward and the suspect's name is within this – Bert Hay. Clue 11: There is a domed building with "Temperance" Billiard Hall 17 "Tables" on it which gives the name of the next suspect to remove – Bill Iard. Clue 12: There is a "railway" "bridge" with the number 2/17 on it which is B and Q "to the letter" which gives the "initials" of the next suspect – Bobby Quinn. Clue 13: There is a "fine symmetrical" building on the right which has the "date" 1909 on it which is S and I "to the letter" which are the "initials" of the next innocent person to remove – Sharon Inghams. Clue 14: There is a blue plaque to "Wandsworth" "Garage" which was a "transport" base. Within the plaque is the name of the next suspect – Don Tram. Clue 15: There is a large black anchor in front of you. This is "contain"ed in the name of the final suspect to remove from the list – Ivan Chord.

Bermondsey Street, Maltby Street Market and Borough Market

Clue 1: There is a "red (read)" "brick" building with the "date" 1903 on it which of you take the numbers "to the letter" is S C which are the "initials" of the next suspect to remove - Simon Carterton. Clue 2: Camarthen Place ("Wales") an "alley" is on the "right" you will find the sculpture "The Shared" ("share") by Austin Emery which "inspires" the name of the next suspect - Emma E Austin. Clue 3: There is another sculpture by Austin Emery who created "The Shared". There is a plaque which mentions different types of "limestone" ("favourite material") which is an anagram ("confusing") of the suspect to remove - Miles Onest. Clue 4: There is a church on the left which has a stone entitled "notice" with various church opening "times" and refers to "divine" service. The rector is Lewen Tugwell which is an anagram ("mixed up") of the next suspect to remove - Gwen Le Tuwell. Clue 5: There is a water ("thirsty") fountain dated 1859 ("nineteenth century") which was a "gift" from Henry Sterry - Terry S. Henry. Clue 6: There is a "blue" plaque in relation to Bermondsey Abbey ("religious instruction") which refers to "Order" of Cluny. The suspects name is based on "Bermondsey Abbey" - Abbie C. Bermond. Culprit: Charlene Wright. She had tried to set up her own bakery up but it had failed and she has been bitter ever since. Clue 7: There is a monument with the names of two churchwardens (and the words "May" and "public") - their last names are Bonny ("pretty") and Grace ("elegant"), respectfully. If they "work together" you get the name of the next suspect to remove - Grace Bonny. Clue 8: There is a "Boys" sign above a "gateway" and a compasses ("direction") symbol on gates on the right hand side of the street which gives the name for the next suspect to remove - Boyce Compass. Clue 9: There is a blue plaque remembering those who died when a "bomb" landed on the air raid "shelter". The "day" this happened is 25 and the month is October (10). If you change these "to the letter: you get Y and J which are the "initials" of the next suspect to remove - Yolande Johnson. Clue 10: There is a stone remembering Griffith Griffiths ("the beginning is sometimes the same" "name"). There is an inscription in Welsh ("language") and "within" that is the suspect's name - Ria Dyn. Clue 11: There is a sign "Guinness Trust" on one of the buildings. The suspect's name is "within" - Ness Trus. Clue 12: You pass Bowling Green Place and Tennis Street ("sporting"). You then see a building on the right which has a plaque to John Marshall on one of the houses where he lived which mentions "spot" and "charity". His name "sounds like" that of the next suspect who is innocent - Ron Partial. Clue 13: There is a memorial to those that passed in the First Wold War showing planes ("flying"). The inscription mentions "Saint Saviour's". The suspect to take off the list is "within" the inscription ("parishioner") - Rishi Oner. Clue 14: There is a "weathered" "grave""stone" with a picture of a shield and the words Smith on it - Rock Shieldsmith. Clue 15: There is a "blue" plaque remembering John Keats and Henry Stephens mentioning "chemist" and "Guys" and St. "Thomas" hospital. The suspect's name reflects the name of one o these poets – Stephen Henrys.

Barnes

Clue 1: There is a "yellow" "brick" house called "Prospect" House with 1878 on it which is R, G, H "to the letter" which are the "initials" of the first suspect to remove, Rita Green-Hopkins. Clue 2: This image is from Grove House which has a "tower" and "lions" on it. The innocent person's name is an anagram ("mixed up") of this – Rose G. Houve. Clue 3: The "Baptis""T" Church has "stone" memorials on it including to "husband and wife" Charles and Rose Tremain whose first names "together" make the name of the next suspect to remove – Charles Rose. Clue 4: The "open" "space" Barnes "Green" is in front of you. The suspect's name is an anagram ("confusion") of this – Breanne Serg. Clue 5: Saint Osmund's Catholic School ("learning") is on the right. There is a "gateway" with two "shields" on it and the "right" one has the "initials" of the next innocent person, S.O.C. – Seamus O'Connor. Clue 6: There is an impressive red-brick building with a "triangle" "pediment" which has the "year" 1905 on it. This is S and E "to the letter" which are the initials of the next suspect to remove – Samira Ebrahim. Culprit: Emilie D. Kramer. She was about to travel to Patagonia on a wildlife trip and wanted a proper lens but could not afford it and saw her chance! Clue 7: "Across the River Thames" is the Emmanuel School "Boat" "Club" which gives the name of the next person to remove from the list – Emma Newell. Clue 8 4 ("for") the "Terrace" is a building with a plaque mentioning "S.""J.""W." and Victoria Cottage. The suspect's name is "within" – Victor I. Acott. Clue 9: There is a house with a "blue" plaque on it to Gustav Holst that was a "compose""r" that composed "The Planets". Gustav Holst is an anagram ("in order") of the next innocent person's name – Val Tugthoss. Clue 10: There is a Network "Rail" sign under the bridge that gives the "bridge" "number" 7/7 for in the event of any road vehicles "striking" the bridge which "to the letter" is G.G. which are the "initials" of the next suspect to remove – Gordon Greenway. Clue 11: There is a building with a "tower" on the right which has the "year" 18"99" on it. If you take this to the letter it is R, I, I which are the "initials" of the next suspect to remove – Robert-Ian Illas. Clue 12: There are silver discs "beneath" your feet which you will "tread" on relating to the "Barnes" "Trail". This is an anagram ("topsy turvy") of the next suspect's name – Talia R. Berns. Clue 13: There is a very pretty cottage called The Beehive ("honey", "insect" "buzzing") on your left – Bea Hyve. Clue 14: There is a house with "arch"ed "windows" call Park View which "sounds like" the name of the next person who can be removed – Marc Pew. Clue 15: There is a house names Roseacre ("smelling of..." "large area") on the left which give you the name of the last suspect – Rowe Saker.

Clapham

Clue 1: There is a plaque "present"ed by Alexander Glegg, the Mayor ("mare") of Wandsworth on the Clock ("time") Tower and the suspect's name is "within" – Lex Anderg. Clue 2: There is a cattle ("not" "human") "t""r""ough" Metropolitan

Drinking ("refreshment") "Fountain" provided by the Cattle Trough "Associa-tion". The next suspect is an anagram ("mixed up") of "Cattle Trough" – Grace Thuttol. Clue 3: There is another fountain ("parched") on the common which was a "gift" of the United Kingdom "Temperance" & "General" "Provide"nt In-stitution. The name of the next suspect is "within" – Al Provid. Clue 4: There is a "year", 1883 on the "Windmill" Hotel ("stay") which is R, H and C "to the letter" which gives the "initials" of the next suspect – Roger Hunt-Clyde. Clue 5: The bandstand ("music") is on the left which is an anagram ("in order") of the next suspect to remove – Stan B. Dand. Clue 6: On Cedars Road there is a blue plaque to the musician Edvard Grieg which says he was a Norwegian "compose"r that "stay"ed here when "perform"ing in London – Greg I. Edvard. Clue 7: There is a blue plaque to "Angel"a" Carter who is a "writ""er" and the next suspect's name is an anagram ("confusion") - Glen A. Certara. Culprit: Oli Takely. He had auditioned for the Chris Martin spot in Luke Warm Play but been told he was too overweight for the role. Clue 8: Further along the road is another blue plaque to Japanese ("far" "east") "novel"ist Natsume Soseki – Nat Sume. Clue 9: At the junction of Cedars Road and Clapham Common North Side is another blue plaque to Sir Charles Barry, "architect" who lived and died here and the suspect's name is "within" – Les Barr. Clue 10: There is a theatre ("play" "drama") on the left and the suspect's name is within the inscription "Erected ("build") A.D. 1889 – Ted Adib. Clue 11: There is another "Drink"ing Fountain & Cattle ("C""ow") Trough Association trough here and the next suspect's name is "within" – Catt Let. Clue 12: There is a house with a "blue" plaque on it to John Francis "Bentley" "Architect" – Francis John. Clue 13: There is a rather fine mansion block with images of the "sea" ("boat", "fish") called Maritime House – Marie Thyme. Clue 14: Oddfellows ("Strange people") Hall, which was a Baptist chapel ("location to pray") has the "year" A.D. 1852 on it which if you take "to the letter" is R, E and B, the "initials" of the next innocent person – Rodney Evans-Bowes. Clue 15: St. Peter's Church ("godly inspiration", "saint") is on the left. On the "left" side "above" the side "door" is a "circle" containing the letters, I, H and A which are the "initials" of the next suspect – Iain Harris-Adam.

Stratford and Hackney Wick

Clue 1: There is a red "steam" train ("rails", "ride") which has Avonside Engine Company on it. The suspect is an anagram ("mixed up") of Avonside Engine ("discount" "company") – Denise E. Avoning. Clue 2: The "London" Aquatics "Centre" ("swimming") is on your left. It shares the same initials as the suspect to remove – Lee-Alan Combe. Clue 3: Sadler's "Well"s, the "dance" company, is on your right and the next suspect's name is an anagram ("confused") of this – Darell S. Slews. Clue 4: There is information about 6.7 million "voice"s which "cheer"ed here in 2012 and the suspect's name is "within" – Milli Onvo. Clue 5: The new V&A Storehouse and Museum ("cultural") is on the opposite bank with a large V&A "sign". V and A are the "initials" of the next suspect – Violette Amand. Clue 6: There are markings on the "ground" showing Greg Rutherford's "jump" for "gold". The suspect's name is "within" – Ruth Erfor. Clue 7: Carpenters ("wood" "work") "Road" "Lock" is in front of you. The next suspect's name is an anagram ("in order") – Spence Tarr. Clue 8: The Olympic Bell ("ring") has an engraving on it including "full of" and "noises". It also has "Be not affeard" which has the suspect's name within – Ben Otaf. Culprit: August B. Edwards. His close friend, Andy, had lost his place in the 200m due to injury and there was a risk Damon would get Andy's Olympic games spot. Clue 9: There are "brick" "pillar""s" and on the ground there are four ("for") "qualities", determination, inspiration, courage and equality. The suspect's name is "within" – Mina T. Ionin. Clue 10: The Paralympics Agitos sculpture which consists of red ("read"), "blue" and "green" shapes is next to the bridge and the suspects name "contains" this - Sakura G. Itoshi. Clue 11: The "copper" "box" arena is on the left with the RUN sculpture ("better not..."). These are the "initials" of the next suspect – Richard Unwin-Newton. Clue 12: The "barriers" are "engraved" with the winners of 2012 Olympics and Paralympics. Opposite "Gate ""B" you will find the name of the person who achieved "silver" in the "Men"'s "TT" "11" "200 m", Daniel Silva "who you are is what you achieve". Within his name is the name of the next suspect to remove – Niel Sil. Clue 13: "Gate" "D" is for Away ("go, go go,...) "support"ers. The next suspect's name is an anagram ("in order") of this – Posy-Sue Partraw. Clue 14: The "large" Orbit "structure" is on the left. The suspects name "contains" this – Corbi Thomas. Clue 15: A "University" "College" "London" or UCL building is on the right and this "sounds like" the name of the last suspect to remove – Lucy Bell.

Highbury and Canonbury

Clue 1: The Union Chapel ("heavenly place") has a plaque on it saying "found"ed in 1799, built 1806 and rebuilt 1877. There are two pastors ("pasta") listed - Thomas Lewis and Henry Allon and you are looking for the "first""name"s of both to eliminate your first suspect - Thomas Henry. Clue 2: The Estorick "Col-lect"ion of Modern Italian "Art" ("creative") is on the right which gives the name of the next suspect to remove - Rick Esto. Clue 3: Canonbury Square Gardens were described as London's most beautiful square by the "Evening" "Standard" in the 1950s. Henry Leroux "start"ed "build"ing here in the 1950s and the suspect's name is an anagram ("mixed up") of this - Roxy-Lee Ruhn. Culprit: Hannah Crowther. She had recently retired and found it difficult to live off her small pension. She thought she could make a considerable amount of money from the book. Clue 4: There is a "green" plaque to "George" "o""r""well" on house number 27 of the square. "Within" the wording on the plaque is the name of the next suspect to remove - Liv Edher. Clue 5: There is a "blue" plaque to Sir Basil ("herb") "Spen""ce". Within the plaque is the suspect's name - Rita Ges. Clue 6: You have reached the New River Walk. The suspect's name is around "New River" ("novel", "flows") - Jane Wrivert. Clue 7: Rose ("flowers", "smelling the..") Villa is on the right on Grange Grove. The next suspect's name "sounds like" this Joe Stiller. Clue 8: There is a shield with a "cross" and a "lion" on it and the motto "deus "per" omnia" on Elizabeth Kenny house and the suspect's name is within - Beth Kenn. Clue 9: There is a clock ("time") "tower" with an inscription on it mentioning Alfred Hutchinson who "presented" the clock tower to the Islington Vestry. The next innocent person is "within" - Fred Hutchins. Clue 10: There is a green plaque to Sir Francis Ronalds "invent"or and pioneer of "electric" "tele""graphy" - Ronald S. Francis. Clue 11: There is a "stone" mentioning "Loyal" "Pride" of Islington Lodge that refers to M.K. Matthews as "architect". The suspect's name is "within" the inscription - Al Prid. Clue 12: There is a green plaque to Charles W. Bower who is a veteran of the "print"ing trade union "movement" and the suspect's name is "within" - Les W. Bowering. Clue 13: There is a plaque marking the Danny Fiszman Bridge and mentioning his "immense contribution" and that he was a "director" and "fan". The next suspect to remove has a name that "sounds like" this - Jan E. Wisman. Clue 14: The Islington Central Library ("book", "borrowed") is on the right. It has Spenser and Bacon ("bring in the...") statues on it - Spenser Bacon. Clue 15: There is a "grave" in St Mary Magdalene Church ("divine inspiration") of the soap ("clean" and "lather") maker John Williams – William Johns.

Broadway Market and Hackney

Clue 1: The London Fields Lido is across the park ("dive", "refreshing") and the suspect's name is "around" "lido" - Kelli Donavan. Clue 2: The Pub in the Park ("place to take refreshment") is on Eleanor Road ("short" "street"). This is an anagram ("mixed up") of the next suspect to remove - Leonard Oroe. Clue 3: There is a "circle" on a house on the left with "London Fields, Hackney, E9". The bottom row, E9 help give the "initials" of the next suspect, E.I. (9 is I if you take it "to the letter") - Emma Isleworth. Clue 4: The Hackney Town Hall is in front of you with a clock ("time") and "shield" on it. The next suspect is an anagram ("confused") of Hackney Town Hall - Hanna-Kelly Wotch. Clue 5: The Hackney Empire ("emperor"), a theatre ("drama") is on the left. The year 1901 is on the building which is S and A "to the letter". These are the initials of the next suspect who is innocent – Samuel Allen. Clue 6: In St "Thomas"'s "Square" there is a fountain ("drink") which has an engraving with the suspect's name "within" – Liam Ham. Clue 7: In St Thomas' Square there is a plaque which mentions Cordwainers Court being "open"ed by H.R.H "Princess" "Royal". The suspect's name is "within" Cordwainers Court – Dwaine R. Scour. Clue 8: There is a red-brick building with a picture of an "oak" and the word "founded". The year is 1710 which is Q and J "to the letter" which are the "initials" of the suspect to remove – Quentin Jackson. Clue 9: There is a building with a stone with "1932" on it which has four letters on it. The "first and second", G and A are the "initials" of the relevant suspect – Gerald Anderson. Clue 10: There is a cattle trough ("bull", "flow"). The suspect's name is within the inscription – Cat Tletro. Clue 11: The "Northside" Studios ("recording") are next to the canal. The next suspect's name to remove is an anagram ("mixing") of Northside – Ron Diseth. Clue 12: You are on the Cat & Mutton "bridge" as indicated by the stones which is an anagram ("mixed up") of the next innocent person – Mona T. Ductant. Culprit: Lucia Borghoni. Billy had stolen her original pitch which had massively impacted her earning potential. Clue 13: On the right is a building with the sign "Sir Walter Scott rebuilt 1909" – Scott Walter. Clue 14: The Dove ("peaceful", "tranquil", "flying) is on the right and the suspect's name is "around" this – Ruth Edoven. Clue 15: There is a school ("education") which has "girls", "boys" and "infants" above the "gates". The suspect's name is an anagram ("confusion") of these words – Ginny-Flossi Brast.

Wapping

Clue 1: There is a plaque in the station stating that this is the "first" "tunnel" for public traffic ever to be "driven" "beneath" a "river". The suspect's name is "within" the name of the "designer" Isambard Kingdom Brunel - Sam Bard. Clue 2: The "Prospect" of Whitby ("wit""by") pub is on your right. The "year" it "start"ed was 1520 which "to the letter" are O and T. These are the "initials" of the next suspect to remove - Omar Tajid. Clue 3: The Pelican ("bird", "crossing") Stairs ("steps") are next to the Prospect of Whitby pub and go down to the Thames where there is a rather sinister noose... The next suspect's name is "within" Pelican - Eli Can. Clue 4: Just after the bridge there is a plaque commemorating site of "Drill" Hall of the 26th Middlesex Volunteers later part of 17th Battalion London Regiment (Poplar and Stepney Rifles) of whom 1,022 soldiers were killed in the "Great" "War" of 1914 to 1918. The suspect's name is "within" the inscription - Reg Imen. Clue 5: The Rotherhithe Ventilation Shaft ("fresh air") has "windows" with LCC on them which is the name of the next suspect - Elsie Seegh. Clue 6: There is a memorial to a group of "explore"rs and "navigat"ors that "sail"ed from Ratcliff "Cross". There are two brothers listed, Stephen and William Borough - William Stephen. Clue 7: On the church there are inscriptions to the "architect" J. Walters and the "build"er R. Streather. If you put these two names together you get the suspect - Walter Streather. Clue 8: The culprit's name is an anagram of Tobacco ("smoke") "Dock" which is in front of you - Coco T. Doback. Clue 9: There is a blue plaque to William Bligh who lived in a house on this site and "transport"ed "bread""fruit" from Tahiti to the West Indies. The suspect's name is "within" - Liam Blig. Clue 10: There is a stone in a building on the left with an inscription that it was laid on the "Festival" of S. Peter and "Glory" to God in the "advancement" of his holy church. W.H. Martin and F.W. Paice are mentioned at the bottom which together gives the name of the next suspect to remove - Martin Paice. Clue 11: The pub called Turner's "Old" "Star" is named after Joseph Turner, the famous "painter" who set up the pub and installed his mistress Mrs "Booth" as proprietor as disclosed by the board talking about his "secret" life - Joe Turner. Clue 12: There is a sign relating to St ("saint") Joan of Wapping "school" which says girls fifty, boys sixty ("numbers"). The latter ("ignore the girls") gives the name of the next suspect to remove - Boyce Ickstie. Culprit: Pierre Montague. He had spent all of his student loan and borrowed money to buy microbrewing equipment and saw the camera as a chance to clear his debts. Clue 13: There is a plaque about Orient ("far east") Wharf developed by Wapping "Steps" Limited and opened by the Bishop of "Step"ney. The innocent person to remove sounds like his name, Jim Thompson - Tim Brompson. Clue 14: The Marine Police HQ has a plaque mentioning that they have "patrol"led the waters for "over 200 years". The suspect's name is an anagram ("mixed up") of Marine Police - Caroline Pime. Clue 15: Phoenix ("fly" and "fire") Wharf is on the left. "Phoenix" is "contain"ed within the last suspect's name - Phoebe Nixon.

Belsize Park

Clue 1: There is a "blue" plaque to Robert Polhill Bevan, a "Camden Town" group " paint"er and the suspect's name is "within" - Bert Pol. Clue 2: There is an engraving lecture ("teaching') "room" above one of the buildings attached to the church ("divine"). The suspect's name is an anagram ("confusion") of this - Cleo Morture. Clue 3: There is a "mansion" "block" on the left called Rosslyn Court ("royalty") - Ross Lyn. Clue 4: The Royal Free Hospital ("medical assistance") is on the right. The suspects name is "within" - Alf Reehos. Culprit: Daphne Pine. She had worked with Chris before when she was younger, turning down a role in a popular soap to do so. Chris had cut her part from the play at the last minute in her eyes ruining her chance for a big break. Clue 5: There is a badge with a "crown" and "white" and "red" "rose"s and the suspect's name is within the motto, "honi soit qui mal 'y pense" - Aly Pen. Clue 6: There is a plaque commemorating the "open"ing of a "day" "nurse""ry" containing "H.R.H." which are the "initials" of the next suspect to remove - Hamish Rupert Henderson. Clue 7: There is a "monument" in South End Green and around it various quotes from famous writers are engraved in the flagstones. One of these writers is Agatha Cristie ("mystery" writer) who "inspires" the name of the next suspect to remove - Chris T. Agaffa. Clue 8: Keats "House", home of the famous "writer" is on the left. It is an anagram ("in order") of the next suspect to remove - Kate Ushose. Clue 9: Jim Henson who created "The Muppets" (Miss "Piggy" and Kermit the "Frog") house is on the left marked by a blue plaque. The next suspect's name "sounds like" this - Tim Benson. Clue 10: There is a police station ("follow the rules") on the left with the "year" "1913" engraved in the stone which if you translate "to the letter" is S and M, the initials of the next suspect who is innocent - Sunita Mani. Clue 11: The imposing building is the Town Hall which has windows which are "circle" shaped. The suspect's name is an anagram ("scrambled") - Walt Lohn. Clue 12: There is a "well" with stonework from the House of "Common"s presented by Mr and Mrs Lionel Barnett. The suspect's name is "within" and "backwards" - Able Noil. Clue 13: The library ("reading", "information") is on the corner which is an anagram ("confused") of the next suspect's name – Barry Li. Clue 14: There is an imposing red brick building on the left of the street with "W.C.A." just left of and above the door. This gives the initials of the next suspect who did not commit the crime - Wendy Casper Adams. Clue 15: The relevant house is "thirt""y" "six" and there are two rather scary looking dogs carved on the door frame. This inspires the name for the last suspect - Kaye Nein.

Hampstead

Clue 1: The "grave" of John Constable ("artist" "policeman") is in St John's "Church" and the name of the suspect to remove is an anagram of this – Jonathon Scelb. Clue 2: There is a blue plaque to the "act"or" Alistair Sim. The suspect's name is "within" this and "backwards" – Ria T. Sal. Clue 3: There is a blue plaque to Kathleen Ferrier the "contra""alt""o" ("sing") which is an anagram ("in order") of the name of the next suspect - Katherine Ferrel. Clue 4: There is a plaque commemorating Robert Louis Stevenson the author ("right" sounds like "write", "Treasure Island" and "Kidnapped" were written by him). The suspect's name is within - Rob Ertlo. Culprit: Lydia Armitage. Making wreaths wasn't making enough to fulfil her ambition of opening a chain of florists and she had been inspired by her partner's highwaymen stories. Clue 5: On the left is "St" "M""ary's" Catholic Church ("time to pray"). There is an inscription ("writing on the wall") on the church and the next suspect's name is "within" - Lena Domin. Clue 6: There is a "blue" "sign" to Sir Henry Dale the "physiolog""ist". The suspect's name is an anagram - Shirley Daner. Clue 7: The "National" "Trust" property Fenton House is on the left which "sounds like" the next innocent person to remove from the list - Ben Tonlowce. Clue 8: There is a plaque to "George" Du Maurier. The next suspect "sounds like" the "last" "name" - Sue Laurier. Clue 9: There is a plaque to the "novel"ist and playwrite ("play" "right") John Galsworthy and the next innocent suspect's name is "within" - Al Swort. Clue 10: The Astronomical Observatory & Meteorological Station ("stars", "space") is on the right and the suspect's name is "within" – Mica Lobser. Clue 11: There is a building on your right with a blue plaque on it to William Hesketh "Lever", the "1st" Viscount Leverhulme who was a "soap"maker. He shares his "initials" with the suspect – Wendy Howell-Lough. Clue 12: The house of Thomas Smith Tait, "architect" is on your left which is an anagram ("in order") of the name of the next suspect – Matt Hamish Tosit. Clue 13: Toll ("price") "Gate" House which was erected to collect tolls from those "passing through" the Western "entrance" to the "estates" of the Bishops of London is on the right and the suspect's name is "within" – Ollga Teho. Clue 14: There is a blue plaque to D. H. Lawrence, "novel""ist" and "poet" – Lawrence Deaiche. Clue 15: The "Well"s and Campden Baths and "Wash" ("soak") Houses 1888 ("three fat ladies" the bingo call) are on the right and the suspect's name is "within" – Den Bathsan.

Notes

Printed in Great Britain
by Amazon